## ADVANCE PRAISE FOR *BREAKING UP WITH PERFECT*

"Perfection is exhausting at best, defeating at worst. In *Breaking Up with Perfect*, Amy is the trusted friend who comes to help us knock down our walls of fear to rebuild a more doable, sustainable, God-honoring life."

—Lysa TerKeurst, *New York Times* bestselling author of
*The Best Yes* and president of Proverbs 31 Ministries

"If you're thinking your relationship with Perfect is worth keeping, Amy helps you face the truth about Perfect's lyin', cheatin', soul-stealin' ways. If you've made the break, but keep dialing this loser's number for one 'last' call, Amy shows you how much grace, freedom, and joy your life will have—*without Perfect*. As she takes each step alongside you, Amy leads you back to the One and only perfect Love of your life—your Heavenly Father."

—Cheri Gregory, speaker and coauthor of
*The Cure for the "Perfect" Life*

"With wit, warmth, and wisdom, Amy Carroll shows us how to break up with perfection so we can *live* our lives rather than manage them. What a gift!"

—Suzanne Eller, international speaker and author of
*The Mended Heart* and *The Unburdened Heart*

"Whether you play the 'good girl' who tries so hard to please God and impress others, or you fear that no matter what you do, you'll never be good enough—you'll be encouraged by this insightful book. Amy's presence on the pages provides a warm and honest voice that will enable you to stop performing and start forging an authentic and intimate walk with Christ."

—Karen Ehman, Proverbs 31 Ministries speaker and
*New York Times* bestselling author of *Keep It Shut: What to Say, How to Say It, and When to Say Nothing at All* and *LET. IT. GO.: How to Stop Running the Show and Start Walking in Faith*

"What a wonderfully relevant and truth-filled book! Amy does an excellent job of weaving authentic personal stories with great Bible content, as well as thought-provoking, reflective questions. Whether you view yourself as a perfect 'good girl' or an insecure 'never good enough' girl, this book is for you. Highly recommend!"

—Cindy Bultema, speaker and author of *Red Hot Faith*

"As a 'good girl' all my life, I've had a serious love affair with Perfect. It's hurt my family, compromised my health, and been a major barrier in my relationship with God. Amy sets 'good girls' like me free by exposing the lies we believe, the pride that isolates us, and the misguided priorities that often drive us. She also guides the girls who wear a mask of perfection because they think they're never 'good enough,' and she points us all to a Savior who fills our longing to be loved—*perfectly*."

—Melinda Means, speaker and coauthor of *Mothering from Scratch: Finding the Best Parenting Style for You and Your Family*

"If you've ever secretly considered a trial separation from perfect, this is your chance. *Breaking Up with Perfect* is the essential remedy for women who wrestle with any degree of perfectionism and long for authentic freedom. Amy Carroll shares poignant stories and insightful truths that will help women slam the door on perfect and never look back."

—Julie K. Gillies, author of *Prayers for a Woman's Soul*

"Before I read *Breaking Up with Perfect* I didn't think I struggled with perfectionism. But I was convicted—in a good way—on every page. I do blame others when they buck my perfect plan. I do try to impress people and fit in at all costs. Not only was I convicted by Amy's words, I was encouraged with God's truth and equipped to leave this façade behind once and for all. Thank you, Amy, for freeing us from lies of perfectionism and setting us on the crooked, rambling path that is real life."

—Amy Lively, speaker, and author of *How to Love Your Neighbors without Being Weird*

# *Breaking Up with* PERFECT

*Kiss Perfection Good-Bye and Embrace
the Joy God Has in Store for You*

# AMY CARROLL

**HOWARD BOOKS**
AN IMPRINT OF SIMON & SCHUSTER, INC.

New York   Nashville   London   Toronto   Sydney   New Delhi

Howard Books
An Imprint of Simon & Schuster, Inc.
1230 Avenue of the Americas
New York, NY 10020

First Howard Books trade paperback edition July 2015

HOWARD and colophon are trademarks of Simon & Schuster, Inc.

For information about special discounts for bulk purchases, please contact Simon & Schuster Special Sales at 1-866-506-1949 or business@simonandschuster.com.

The Simon & Schuster Speakers Bureau can bring authors to your live event. For more information or to book an event, contact the Simon & Schuster Speakers Bureau at 1-866-248-3049 or visit our website at www.simonspeakers.com.

Manufactured in the United States of America

1   3   5   7   9   10   8   6   4   2

Library of Congress Cataloging-in-Publication Data

Carroll, Amy, 1967–
Breaking up with perfection / Amy Carroll. —First Edition.
     pages cm
1. Self-actualization (Psychology) Religious aspects—Christianity.
2. Women—Psychology. I. Title.
     BV4598.2.C375 2015
     248.8'43 dc23
     2015005273

ISBN 978-1-5011-0295-0
ISBN 978-1-5011-0305-6 (ebook)

To Barry,
who knew I could when I thought I couldn't,
who tenderly loves the whole package—
imperfections included. I love you forever.

# CONTENTS

*Breaking Up with*

# PERFECT

***The Lie of Perfection***

*My list defines me.*

***The Truth of God's Love***

*My list distances me from God and people.*

*Introduction*

# BREAKING UP IS HARD TO DO

## *What Kind of Girl Are You—Good Girl or Never Good Enough?*

I already want us to be friends. But as I sit at my computer to invite you to join me in breaking up with perfectionism, I feel the familiar flutter of insecurity in my stomach. The tightness in my chest scoots in close as if it's an old buddy, and the worries swirling through my brain are shark bait for my greatest fears.

*What if this book isn't good enough for you, and you already know more about leaving this pursuit of perfection than I do? What if you don't like it? What if you don't like me?*

*Wait, I'm not all that messed up . . . am I? Do I really want to let you know how messed up I am?*

I must admit that it's embarrassing to expose my brand of crazy this early in our journey together. But I have to tell you I have a weird dichotomy in my head, one voice saying I'm doing better when it comes to breaking up with perfectionism and another that is overflowing with self-doubt. You see, if we sat down together for a cup of coffee, you wouldn't initially see me as a woman on a journey to live free of the crushing weight of perfection. I come across light, a glass-half-full kind of girl with an optimistic outlook and a cheerful disposition. I love to be silly, laugh, and hang out with friends. I'm willing to tell stories of my failures and foibles, but I'm told I appear confident and unafraid. My outward appearance defies my inner reality. What others perceive as happiness and confidence on the outside is often a jumbled, tangled-up mess inside.

All relationships are complex, but the one with ourselves may be the most so. Although it's hard to read our own hearts accurately, the truth is that none of us is one-dimensional. We're beautifully intricate, and we regularly contradict ourselves. Our complexity is exhausting, isn't it? In fact, if you liked the title of this book enough to be reading it now, I'm guessing you're a lot like me. I can safely say that you are probably weary right down to the core of your bones. The hot pursuit of perfection is wearing you to a nub, and I understand. We girls with shiny exteriors are nothing if not hardworking. We work to look right, act right, think right, and produce, produce, produce.

*All relationships are complex, but the one with ourselves may be the most so.*

Your morning may have started in the gym, whipping your body into shape (or back into shape) before you ran home to cook breakfast, start a load of laundry, and rush out the door to the next thing on your carefully maintained to-do list.

Maybe you're heading to work, where your goals for the day are to finish the best project your boss has ever seen, set an example by not gossiping at lunch, organize your desk, and share Jesus with the woman in the cubicle next door.

Or maybe you're the woman packing your beautiful angels into the minivan, praying nobody you know will see their meltdowns at the grocery store and that their cute new outfits won't get stained at the park. You're home by late afternoon to start cooking dinner for a sick neighbor, scheduling the volunteers for VBS, and scrubbing your toilets to a polished glow.

Whatever life you live, we women enmeshed with perfectionism want to always live up to expectations and never let anyone down. By definition, pleasing ourselves means pleasing and taking care of everybody else. Good things do come our way because of that trait. But there are some downsides too.

Most of the time, we get approval and pats on the back, and we might even have a wall of Employee/Daughter/Mother/Teacher/Wife of the Year plaques. Those are the things that keep us going . . . most of the time. But in the quiet moments, the fatigue sets in, and we realize those kudos haven't fueled us at all. In those times of true reflection, if we're honest, we feel numb and defeated and hollow.

How did we get to this place where all looks well on the outside but we're starved on the inside? Some lovers of Perfect live with the *Good Girl Syndrome*. These women are rule followers by nature and bask in earning the pleasure of the people surrounding them. Others live with the *Never Good Enough Syndrome*. These women use their flawless exterior to cover the wounds and shame of their pasts. Both kinds of women build an external structure rule by rule and pleasant smile by pleasant smile. We seek to portray our lives as picturesque cottages with English gardens surrounded by white picket fences. But inside, the rooms of our hearts are empty, echoing boxes devoid of the wonderful messiness of deep relationships, love, authenticity, and compassion.

The biggest downside of pursuing perfection is the way it affects *relationships.* I was the little girl who tried so hard to measure up and fit —— in, the typical firstborn child work-

*The biggest downside of pursuing perfection is the way it affects relationships.*

ing to please and achieve. Despite having incredibly loving parents, my inner wiring drove me to try to excel, meet every perceived expectation, and earn the title "exceptional."

But for all my efforts to please others, my relationships were doomed to fall short of what they could have been if I had just felt free to be myself.

After sharing with one woman about my journey to reform, she told me, "I've avoided good girls like you my whole life."

Ha! And who doesn't?! Even as a child, my rule-follower tendencies didn't serve me very well. I had some friends, but I was never the best friend. I was the goody-goody, straitlaced girl other little girls tended to avoid instead of being drawn to. And I was lonely, wondering what was wrong when I was trying so hard . . . until fourth grade, when everything changed because of Josie.

## IDENTIFYING YOUR LIST

Josie was the girl everyone wanted as their friend. She was cute and smart and funny—a triple threat. Everybody sought Josie's friendship, but she chose me. And when Josie made me her friend, my life began to change. Her confidence built my confidence. Our parents were driven to distraction by our constant giggling, and she made me feel brave. The knots in my stomach loosened, and my pet butterflies fluttered away to more nervous tummies.

At that point of innocence and girlhood, we both held tightly to the Good Girl List. You might be acquainted with that list. It's the one we clutch to our hearts that tells us what we have to do to be good enough, to be accepted, and to be loved. I guess we all have slightly different items to check off on our Good Girl Lists, but we probably have a lot in common. For fourth-grade girls, the list reads something like this:

- Do what your parents tell you.
- Keep everyone happy.
- Make good grades.
- Smile at everybody so they'll think you're nice.
- Wear what everyone else wears.
- Be nice to your friends . . . and everyone else.
- Make sure everyone likes you.
- Share.
- Make sure everybody sees your good deeds.
- Go to church.
- Don't be *too* mean to your little brother. (He deserved it sometimes. I wasn't *that* good!)

Sound familiar? It's the list you make so everyone will like you and be your friend. But it's also the list that turns to bite you by creating superficial friendships while you hide your flaws or by driving others away because of your unattainable image. It's the list that stokes the ache of loneliness even in the press of a crowd.

Josie and I were bonded by our Good Girl Lists, but then came high school, where Josie found herself saddled with a new list: the Never Good Enough List. As the bad choices accumulate and the Never Good Enough List grows, many former Good Girls, like Josie, drop their old Good Girl Lists in defeat. Other girls start out with this list from a very young age—often because they feel their parents' displeasure (real or imagined) early on or because of abuse or neglect. Whenever this list begins and for whatever reasons, it seems to grow item by item:

- No matter what I do, I can't please my parents.
- People always disapprove of me.
- I'm not smart enough to achieve my dreams.
- If I smile, I can hide how I really feel.
- I'll try, but I'll never fit in.
- No one likes me. I'm unlovable.
- My bad choices make me a bad person.
- I don't have anything good to offer.
- I am invisible.
- Church makes me feel guilty.

Whether the origins of the Never Good Enough List are the hurtful things others did to us or our own bad choices, the list begins to define us and serves to separate us from God's love.

Though not everyone follows the same pattern that Josie did, Josie eventually resigned from the Good Girl club and relabeled herself as Never Good Enough. Maybe this has been your experience too.

Josie and I never had a big blowup. There wasn't a huge conflict or confrontation, but our paths began to diverge. Our relationship disintegrated. Although we loved each other, our tightly held lists created a seemingly unbridgeable divide. Our friendship story wasn't over, but it stayed in a holding pattern of near estrangement for a long, long time.

Here's the crucial truth we both learned in our journey on divergent paths: both lists are equally destructive. While the Good Girl List is a long inventory of all we *need to do* to earn God's love, the Never Good Enough List chronicles all the reasons we'll *never be able* to earn His love. The same item that one Good Girl adds to her list as something to aspire to (like "I must make sure everyone likes me") may be posted to the Never Good Enough List as another's proof of her unworthiness ("No one could ever like me"). While both women measure themselves by an unyielding standard of perfection, they come at their lists from different entry points—one continually strives to *do*; the other is completely convinced she never *can*. Both lists keep our hearts disengaged from the deep, authentic relationships for which we were created and away from the joy of living our truest self.

Perfect is kind of like that bad boyfriend who's hard to get rid of. He was so eye-catching at first, and we loved everything about him. He had an irresistible draw, and we pursued him relentlessly, investing all our efforts and emotions in him. But slowly, over time, that old boy-

> *Both lists keep our hearts disengaged from the deep, authentic relationships for which we were created and away from the joy of living our truest self.*

friend lost his allure, and so does Perfect. What looked like love begins to be a burden, and as the initial infatuation wears off, the relationship begins to grate on us. It wasn't what we thought or hoped for at all. Finally, we start to realize that what seemed so wonderful is actually destructive. So how in the world do we break up with Perfect when we've longed for and pursued it for so long? How do we disentangle ourselves when our onetime crush stalks us like an unrequited love?

## THE BROKEN PERSONALITY OF THE GOOD GIRL

For some, the Good Girl List is one that a parent or other influence in your life developed and enforced. But for many of us, including myself, it's simply a function of personality. We lean toward perfectionism and meticulousness while lacking the ability to flex or extend grace (mostly to ourselves). Good Girls tend to be wound tight with a heightened sensitivity to any perceived slight or disapproval. We can be nervous by nature, task-driven, and afraid to take leaps of faith. Recognize any of those traits in yourself?

One personality trait I've exhibited since I can remember is an overdeveloped sense of responsibility. I have loved being known as responsible, the "go-to girl" who can always be relied on to do the task right and on time. Although it's positive to take responsibility, it's terrible to feel a sense of full responsibility for everything around you. As a little girl, I remember feeling shame for anything from cutting paper incorrectly in art class to the other girls in my group piano lessons misbehaving. Was some of it truly my fault or responsibility? Yep. Should I have taken it all onto my shoulders? Nope.

And yet, years later, as a woman in my forties, I found myself melting down during a ministry conference with that same extreme sense of over-responsibility. Early in the morning, I was filled with excitement as I arranged the display on the table for a coaching service I was launching. *I can't wait to see how the women respond!* I thought as I surveyed the display. Since it looked a little sparse, I headed over to our resource table to borrow a few books for a bit more decorating. *Hmmm ... there's nobody here to ask for permission, but it's all right, since I'll just return them at the end,* I reasoned.

Later that day when I returned to the table from a break, I was horrified to see that the borrowed books had disappeared. Where had they gone? To this day, I believe that attendees, assuming they were free samples, picked them up and tucked them into conference book bags as they walked by.

That night I was inconsolable. As my feelings roller-coastered, my thoughts swirled in an endless downward spiral. *Everyone is going to be so disappointed in me. Maybe they'll think I just lost them. Those books were worth hundreds of dollars, and I can't pay it. I'm* sure *they'll make me pay it!*

My friend in leadership tried to reassure me that it wasn't my fault and that the ministry wouldn't hold me responsible. Three times I interrupted and repeated, "But if I had only marked them 'Not for Sale.' If I hadn't borrowed them ... If I had stayed at the table ..."

"It's not your responsibility," my friend patiently repeated over and over. Finally, exasperated with my agonizing, she repeated a final time, "*In the name of Jesus, it is not your responsibility!*" My out-of-control distress broke, and we both dissolved in giggles.

I believe my personality has gotten me off track in ways such as this from the day I was born. How else do you explain a girl growing up in a loving, accepting family having such an overdeveloped sense of responsibility? I could tell other stories with harsher outcomes, but the bottom line is that I was using responsibility to drive myself relentlessly in order to look good to others. This ambition amped up my emotions beyond reason, but nothing is worth putting ourselves under that much pressure. Nothing, nada, zilch. That's why we so desperately need God to free us.

So if we're bound up in parts of our personalities, what are we to do? The bad news is that our personalities are very ingrained, and some theorists say they are set from the time we are six years old. The good news is that God created us as whole individuals, personalities and all! And we know that in Him and through Him, all things are possible, even changes in the expressions of how we are wired. Both Good Girls and Never Good Enough Girls can overcome flaws in our personalities that bind us to our lists.

Several years ago, our Proverbs 31 ministry team used a book called *StrengthsFinder 2.0* to identify the strengths of our personalities. I read the book, completed the online evaluation, and received my list of strengths. My top three were belief, discipline, and responsibility. Imagine my relief and angst that responsibility was at the top of that list! Reading the descriptions, I realized the evaluation described me almost exactly. And yet I despaired.

Just the week before, I had responded to a hurting friend in a very black-and-white, abrupt way. My desire was to help with what I perceived as truth, but it was not the response my precious friend needed in the midst of her heartbreak. Although I may have had an accurate insight, it came across as cold, judgmental, and self-righteous. Her justified reaction of hurt molded the way I started to see myself. All I could recognize were the downsides of my strengths, and this is how it translated in my mind:

Responsibility = Cold
Discipline = Judgmental
Belief = Self-righteous

Even the book confirmed that for every strength there is a down-side, but all I could see in the period of grief over how I had hurt my friend were my weaknesses. In my prayer times, I began to wrestle with God. "This is not the woman I want to be," I complained. "Please change me," I begged. Repentance—being sorry for sin—is a good thing, but I had already asked both my friend and God for for-

*That morning I crossed over into accusing my Creator of making a mess when He made me.*

giveness. That morning I crossed over into accusing my Creator of making a mess when He made me.

Here's how God *could* have replied: "You turn things upside down, as if the potter were thought to be like the clay! Shall what is formed say to him who formed it, 'You did not make me'? Can the pot say to the potter, 'You know nothing'?" (Isaiah 29:16).

But that morning, God was very gentle with me. In the loudest thought, God spoke into my heart and mind and said, "Amy, I'm so sorry you don't like the way I made you, but I am *delighted* with you."

What heart-piercing words! Even as I type those words on my computer, my eyes well up with tears at His grace, love, and mercy. I want to turn those words around to you.

"Daughter, I am *delighted* with you."

Are we flawed? Oh, yes. Because sin entered the world when Adam and Eve disobeyed God at the beginning of time, each of us has a built-in sin nature that warps even our God-given personalities. Listen closely to me, though. God made us perfectly in His image to reflect Himself. Whether you are a woman with Never Good Enough Syndrome or Good Girl Syndrome, you are completely loved, accepted, and delighted in.

When I'm studying Scripture, I love to read a trustworthy word-for-word translation, like the New International Version, alongside a newer thought-for-thought translation like The Message or the New Living Translation. Reading familiar scriptures in a new form often jolts my heart into hearing them as if I'd never heard them before. On the day I was struggling to see myself as God's delightful creation, I needed to let Psalm 139 reset my heart. Let this familiar passage from The Message version soak into your soul in a fresh way:

> *Oh yes, you shaped me first inside, then out;*
> *you formed me in my mother's womb.*
> *I thank you, High God—you're breathtaking!*
> *Body and soul, I am marvelously made!*
> *I worship in adoration—what a creation!*
> *You know me inside and out,*
> *you know every bone in my body;*
> *You know exactly how I was made, bit by bit,*
> *how I was sculpted from nothing into something.*
> *Like an open book, you watched me grow from conception to birth;*
> *all the stages of my life were spread out before you.*
> *The days of my life all prepared*
> *before I'd even lived one day.*

(Psalm 139:13–16, The Message)

We are beautifully created: first inside (our personalities, our minds, and our emotions), then outside (our bodies). Our personalities may be or become flawed—just like our bodies—but it is equally true that our personalities can be redeemed. Without Jesus, there is no hope for overcoming the weaknesses in our personalities, but with Jesus, our beautiful Redeemer, there is great hope. With Jesus, our God-created personalities can become the beautiful centerpieces of our souls they are intended to be.

I've fallen into the trap of being dissatisfied with what God gave me, but I've learned that I can turn around my perceived weaknesses into opportunities to identify with other women in the same places. The goody-goody girl from my younger years is gone, and she's been replaced by an "I can see where you're coming from" girl people don't mind being around—a girl who puts herself on the same level as everyone else and offers encouragement out of who God made her to be. God can truly take us from sharp-edged goody-goody to grace-filled friend. It makes my heart soar to know that not only is personality refinement possible, it is part of God's restorative plan for me.

## OUR BROKEN PASTS AND THE NEVER GOOD ENOUGH SYNDROME

For some of us—especially the Never Good Enough Girls—perfectionism is more a learned behavior than a personality trait. It's the way we've reinvented ourselves to hide or compensate for a past we'd rather forget. Even women who look like they've been on the straight and narrow have places of regret and shame in their past. But for Never Good Enough women, their pasts have created a negative relationship with themselves that's hard to break. I've listened, brokenhearted, as friends have shared story after painful story of abuse, rejection, loss, and devastating choices. In the timbre of each woman's voice, I heard a little girl crying out for love, acceptance, and nurturing.

The source of this pain seems to be one of two distinct origins: the pain inflicted by someone else's sin or the pain we create for ourselves by our own bad choices. While Good Girls may struggle with their personality quietly and privately, the consequences of the past that Never Good Enough Girls struggle with are external, loud, and humiliating. The shame and public nature of the fallout is part of what forms the Never Good Enough List. This list chronicles all the reasons we'll *never be able* to earn God's love.

As adults, it's the effort to hide our shameful pasts behind the façade of perfection that can keep us from living a life of freedom and fulfilling friendships. Even if we have been rescued by God's grace, it's easier to give mental assent to forgiveness than to step into true liberation. The Never Good Enough list makes us prone to despair and giving up.

I think about a friend we'll call Sarah who shared in whispers the terrible names her father called her when she was a little girl as he commented at family meals about her weight. Those same names echo in her adult mind anytime she feels she's falling short. It's her father's voice of rejection and ridicule ringing in her ears that makes her afraid to reach out and connect in deep friendships. Although the abuse was clearly her father's sin, Sarah's past keeps her isolated and ashamed. Even so, she hides her pain well as she excels in her work and as a mother. She's created a life that looks carefree and perfect on the outside, while she hides the deep wounds from her past on the inside.

Maybe you relate to Sarah. The very people who should have loved, nurtured, and encouraged you as a child denigrated you instead. Perhaps physical or sexual abuse ties you to the feeling that you'll never be able to measure up. Maybe neglect or verbal abuse has created voices of unworthiness in your head that seem impossible to silence. Maybe you have created an outward persona of perfection, hoping no one will blast past the walls and get close enough to see how far you fall short. You look just like the woman with the Good Girl List, but your feelings inside are very different.

Or maybe you relate more to my childhood friend Josie, whose own choices led her down a path of never feeling good enough. When I asked her how it felt to take those first steps away from the Good Girl List, she answered, "When you're acting out, you always feel bad and ashamed, because what you're doing goes against everything in you, everything you are." She then followed with this beautiful truth: "I thought I had to be either all good or all bad, so I spent a lot of time running between the lists. But then I realized nobody's all one or all the other. The truth is somewhere in between, in a place we don't control. Now I know that God will meet me exactly where I am."

*The Never Good Enough Girl looks just like the woman with the Good Girl List, but her feelings inside are very different.*

Josie's words are so true. God gently invites us to break up with our past and fall head over heels in love with His offer of grace, nurturing, forgiveness, and healing.

Josie's point is freeing for women who adhere to the Good Girl List and for those who adhere to the Never Good Enough List. God wants to destroy the distance those lists create, so maybe, just maybe, He's destined us to let go of those lists forever. It's the first step to breaking up with Perfect.

## STAGING AN UPRISING

Even though I tend toward being a rule follower, I have a rebel streak too. I hope you have a little rebel in you as well—whether you're a Good Girl like me or struggle with feeling Never Good Enough. Sometimes that rebel streak serves us very well. Just when we feel beaten into submission and nearly subdued by our lists, our inner rebel rises up, our sass kicks in, and fresh strength surges to fight our urge to be perfect!

You might say to me, "Okay, now I'm confused. You're telling me that being good is bad and being rebellious is good?" My answer is a definite "Yes!" Sometimes. When good deeds come from bad motives instead of a pure heart, the Good Girl List becomes a recipe for self-absorption and pride, and the Never Good Enough List shames us into defeat. When this happens, we need to rebel!

My personal rebellious streak is the type that resists mediocrity and staying safe for the sake of comfort. When I feel afraid of taking risks and following a God who wants nothing less than full freedom for me, the rebel in me rises up and inspires me to throw off my conventional, self-imposed restrictions and seek God's heart and mind relentlessly.

When our lists interfere with the gifts God has for us, that's when it's okay to rebel. Not only okay—but good! When we—as freedom-loving women—band together in this uprising, a miraculous thing happens. Restoration begins. Relationships begin to flourish, and these relationships fulfill the profound longing that we all have for deeper love—a love that extends to God, ourselves, and others.

Even though our longing for relationship is God-instilled, we often turn that longing upside down, and it becomes an unhealthy impetus for approval. That upside-down longing is what compelled me to ask you to be my friend at the beginning of this chapter and is what propels us into a frenzy of trying harder and harder to earn love.

But when we participate in this righteous rebellion, our longings are turned right-side up and morph from the warped pursuit of perfectionism to the beauty of authenticity. Instead of seeking perfection, we'll be free to weave ourselves together with God and with the people we love—and the new relationships will be tighter and more real than we've ever imagined. Tighter than all our self-determined work could ever accomplish. And that's what we've been after all along, right?

Josie and I saw this relationship transformation in the restoration of our childhood friendship. We've been reunited as grown women, joined not by our lists but by our Savior. We've rebelled against our lists and handed them over to Jesus, and He has strengthened our precious friendship as well as our souls. I rejoice in the opportunity to join the story of my friendship with Josie to your stories. My prayer is that our intertwined stories will create a beautiful testimony of God's redeeming goodness in our lives, despite our broken attempts at being perfect.

I no longer experience the level of angst I used to shoulder. I'm still very much in process and learning to live a flawed, imperfect, authentic life, but I've come a long, long way toward being truly free.

And so in this book, I want to give you two ways to evaluate where you are today and help you take steps toward breaking up with Perfect for good. First, at the end of each chapter I'll have a few questions for reflection that I call Transformation Points. Because I don't want to add to anybody's list (!!), you can handle these questions in a couple of ways. If you'd just like to use them prayerfully, inviting God into a time of helping you see yourself clearly, you can do that, or you may want to use these questions to start or add to a journal.

And second, because I strongly believe in the power of God's Word, His gift to us called the Bible, I've also included a more extensive study section at the back of the book called "Going Deeper." If you're working with a small group, the "Going Deeper" section is terrific for your discussion time together. Whether you explore this section alone or in a group, I encourage you to take your time and not rush. No matter how much you're able to complete at this stage of your life, I'm trusting God to do the work He had in mind when you picked up this book. I'm so glad we're growing together!

Breaking up with Perfect is hard to do, but what we gain is infinitely superior to what we give up. You and I are created to have real relationships, so let's go on this journey together, trekking far beyond the obstacles of our personalities and pasts toward abundance and delight.

## Transformation Points

1. Which list have you adhered to—the Good Girl List or the Never Good Enough List?

2. How has your list affected the way you live?

3. What makes you want to break up with Perfect?

4. Write a prayer asking God to help you take your first step away from your list and toward Him and the freedom He has for you today.

# Part One

# BREAKING UP WITH
# WRONG BELIEFS

*Getting Free from What Fills Our Heads*

### The Lie of Perfection

*God is a taskmaster who rations out love
in measure with our output.*

### The Truth of God's Love

*God loves me lavishly and wants me to rest in Him.*

*Chapter One*

# WHAT A FOOL BELIEVES

## *Shattering Our False Beliefs About God*

Belief is a funny thing. It determines how we act and react. In the beginning of my marriage, I believed my husband, Barry, was the luckiest man alive. After all, he had married me, a woman who was going to introduce him to one of the principal joys of life: a live Christmas tree. He had grown up in a household with an abomination—an *artificial* Christmas tree. I was going to introduce him to new Christmas traditions and share with him joy untold! So each year we went to the Christmas tree lot to buy a fragrant, bushy, *live* tree. We'd haul it home, put it in the Christmas tree stand filled with water, and decorate that lovely evergreen—as we sang "O Tannenbaum" with lovely smiles on our faces all the while. Okay, so maybe I'm embellishing a little, but suffice it to say, having a live Christmas tree thrilled the HGTV corner of my heart.

There was one thing that made me very unhappy, however. Every Christmas, and I mean *every* Christmas, my darling hubby was sick. The first Christmas I attended to him with newlywed sweetness. The second Christmas, I tolerated him and brought him soup. By the third Christmas of holiday sickness, I was just plain annoyed. What was wrong with the man? He was big and strapping and healthy and nice on the eyes. How could he become so weak and sickly and pitiful every year at Christmas? I began to make snide remarks under my breath about his mysterious seasonal illness, seemingly brought on by exposure to my family.

Sometime in that fourth year, Barry went to the doctor for yet another round of Christmas illness, and the doctor sent him to a specialist who did very extensive tests. This doctor had Barry lie on his stomach while he poked lots and lots of tiny needles in his back. As you may have guessed by now, the test results revealed that my poor husband is allergic to almost every green living thing . . . including Christmas trees.

*Because I believed* that live Christmas trees were far superior to artificial trees, every year we dragged a beautiful, green, bushy death trap into our living room. *Because I believed* Barry just didn't like the holidays, I got snappy with him when he was sick. *Because I believed* the wrong things, I acted in wrong ways. Only when I learned and believed the truth could we step into the mutual joy of an artificial tree complete with attached strings of lights. Hallelujah! The joy of Christmas returned! But I was completely humbled and dismayed to realize how my skewed beliefs had damaged a relationship I treasure.

> **Because I believed the wrong things, I acted in wrong ways.**

## THE ACCIDENTAL IDOL

What we believe about God affects our actions and ultimately our relationship with Him. Our beliefs shape how we feel about God, our place in the world, and the person we will become. If what we believe is the truth about God and His character, then we'll grow into an increasingly close and genuine relationship with Him, becoming more and more the women God intended from the day He dreamed us up. Too often, though, our beliefs about God are based on religious tradition, what other people say about Him, superstition, or simply our own thoughts and perceptions. A distorted concept of God can begin to form in our minds and hearts—a picture that is far from His true character.

When we base our beliefs on false ideas of God, we create a god of our own making. Then we are deceived by our wrong beliefs into investing time, energy, resources, and emotions in this god, convinced we're building a relationship with God Himself. It's possible for our hearts to be in the right place even while we are moving in the wrong direction.

Women with the Good Girl List and those with the Never Good Enough List start with the same core understanding: God is perfect. He is holy, set apart. God is big and powerful and totally different from us. As many have said, God is God and we are not. That truth is a very good thing to know, but so many of us, including myself, start to derail even within the bounds of that foundational truth.

Women with the Good Girl List often derail by creating a false god through the following line of reasoning (this is how my very linear brain works). Their definition of God becomes distorted:

- God is good; therefore, He wants me to be good.
- He is not only good but perfect. He's working in me to perfect me. (So far, so good.)
- God insists I must be perfect in order to be close to Him. (Uh-oh.)
- God will only love me if I am perfect. (Red alert!)
- *Conclusion:* I must work to be perfect so God will love me. (Game over.)

With this definition of God, I've created an idol. Instead of believing in a God who can make me truly good through His transformative grace, I begin to worship a god who will only love me if I'm perfect—*perfect* being defined by my ever-present Good Girl List. When I write out this flawed definition of God, even I can see it's cracked to think this way, but I know from living the Good Girl List myself that this flawed definition of God is hidden in many a Good Girl's heart. It may not be an idol carved from wood, but it's an idol nevertheless, looming large and imposing in the way we think and live. Suddenly, without even realizing it, I'm breaking God's second commandment: "You shall not make for yourself an idol in the form of anything in heaven above or on the earth beneath or in the waters below. You shall not bow down to them or worship them; for I, the LORD your God, am a jealous God" (Exodus 20:4–5a, NIV 1984).

For example, I've believed in a god who wanted me to be cheerful and perennially positive in order to please him. "Be positive" was an item I had written on my Good Girl List. The problem with that belief surfaced during difficult times in my life. With both of my pregnancies, I was extremely sick with a condition doctors call hyperemesis, which loosely translated means "throwing up day and night."

Although I needed God desperately during these months, I withdrew from Him. I had created a god who insisted on a positive attitude instead of a God whom I could trust to carry me through, even when I wasn't feeling so positive. But because I couldn't force cheerfulness and pull myself up by my bootstraps in the midst of my misery, I withdrew from God, thinking He was displeased with me.

That definition of God isn't so different for women with the Never Good Enough List. Their reasoning starts off the same, and only the final conclusion is different.

- God is good; therefore, He wants me to be good.
- He is not only good but perfect. He wants me to be perfect. (So far, so good.)
- God insists I must be perfect in order to be close to Him. (Oh, mercy.)
- God will only love me if I am perfect. (Red alert!)
- *Conclusion:* I'm not perfect, so God will never love me. (Game over.)

Before God straightened her beliefs, my Never Good Enough friend Holly processed her position with God this way: "I believed that as long as I performed well, I would be accepted." It was when she wasn't performing as expected that she ran into problems with her wrong beliefs about God. In college Holly was defiantly pursuing a romance with a young man who didn't share her faith and values. She recounts a story of riding home from a weekend with her college boyfriend and his family while she cried the whole way. "I knew my parents wouldn't approve, and neither would God," she explained. Although she later saw her grief over her bad decisions as proof of God's work in her heart, at the time all she felt was the weight of a shattered relationship. "I believed God was the big, angry man in the sky. He was unapproachable, and my sense of guilt reinforced those beliefs." She believed she was disappointing God, but she didn't want to give up her right to make her own choices. The result was that Holly believed she was unaccepted, thus unloved, by God.

Wrong beliefs about God like Holly's and mine aren't harmless. They actually damage our relationship with God because they lead to doing life without Him, clutching our false god instead of the True God we can trust. To repair the damage, we have to break up with our definition of a god who demands perfection and fall in love with who God says He really is.

When I was in college, my best friend, Anna, and I lived in a duplex beside a very handsome man. Each day we'd watch him leave his apartment in the morning, clad in riding breeches and a starched white shirt, with his wavy blond hair blowing in the breeze—looking as if he was headed for a movie set. Anna and I began to weave a story about him. We imagined the day that he'd knock on the door of our little cinder-block hovel and announce in a deep, rich voice that he had come to take one of us away to his English palace to be his wife. I know it was ridiculous girl stuff, but we had fun making up all kinds of stories about his life as a prince and why he was living beside us in Chapel Hill, North Carolina.

> *Wrong beliefs about God aren't harmless.*
>
> *They actually damage our relationship with Him.*

Then the day came when I actually met the man instead of just watching him from afar. When he opened his mouth to speak, out came a high voice and Southern drawl. My dreams of an English prince came crashing down. Silly, right? If only I had talked to him from the beginning, we might have had a friendship based on who he really was and the truths he told me about himself.

Just like we each want to have the ability to define ourselves as we really are, rather than being defined by how others perceive us, God has the ultimate authority to define Himself as He really is and to give us insight into His character. He's given us the gift of the Bible to tell us the truth about Him, and yet so often we rely more heavily on the stories we've told ourselves. We must turn completely away from these old stories in order to love the new and the true. This redirection is essential, because our imperfect view of God deprives us of God's most miraculous ability—His perfecting work in us.

The Good Girl List and the Never Good Enough List deny who God is. Only He can perfect us. Only He can give us life. Our lists will never accomplish what we hope; they will never bring us love or acceptance. In John 14:6, Jesus is very clear: "I am the way and the truth and the life. No one comes to the Father except through me." As much as we have placed our hope in our lists in the past, we need to see them for the broken methods they are and transfer our hope to Christ alone. As a friend said to me, "Our lists will never give us life."

Attaining perfection, as I've defined it thus far, is a work we try to do ourselves, but *perfecting* us is actually a work that God accomplishes. It's the supernatural work He does within us as we surrender our lists and all of ourselves to Him. Philippians 1:6 says that we can be "confident of this, that he who began a good work in you will carry it on to completion until the day of Christ Jesus." It's God who begins a good work in us—including setting us free from perfect—and He is the only one who can complete it. That's His perfecting power.

## A LITTLE IDOL CRUSHING

For women who try to live by the Good Girl List, our way of thinking leads to a never-ending, soul-crushing cycle of work. Ultimately, our belief that we have to work hard for God's love leads to exhaustion, despair, and eventually numbness. A few years ago, I reached the place of numbness. Although I was in ministry, constantly writing and speaking of God's incomparable love, I couldn't feel that love. Not at all. I started to feel like a ministry machine, only valued by God for what I produced. It took coffee with a faithful, truth-telling friend to jolt me out of my rut.

On the day of our time together, I entered Rey's beautiful home with anticipation of what she'd share with me. I had a deep sense that God had directed me to her and that He was planning to use her words to impact me. I didn't have a clue how deeply those words would pierce. You see, I looked like I had it all together, so I assumed Rey believed I had it all together. We chatted pleasantly for a few minutes, and then she said, "Amy, I believe I have a question for you. I heard you teach a couple of years ago. It wasn't bad teaching; but when you finished, I had a question in my mind. I asked myself, 'If that list of hers, the list of all the things she needs to do to get the result she wants from God, falls apart, will she make it?'"

Rey then began to share her own testimony. She told me how she saw many similarities between us, particularly our rule-following natures. Until a crisis point in her life when things weren't as she'd dreamed, she too had believed that working hard to follow God assured not only His love but His rewards. Then she looked me in the eyes and said, "Amy, God loves you. Unconditionally. There is nothing you can do to earn any more of His love. Even when things start to go wrong, as they will eventually, He will still love you through the hard things. It's all about His grace, Amy, and His grace is a free gift. So if everything goes wrong, will you make it? Will your faith survive?"

I burst into tears. In that moment, I understood how much my list and striving to be perfect had taken over my life. Not just my faith but my life. My stomach churned, and a sick feeling swept over me. I could hardly believe that my issue was so transparent to someone with whom I had shared so little time. The perfect image I thought I'd so carefully constructed was shattered.

God used Rey in that moment to say the exact thing my heart needed to hear. It takes strong, hard truth to crush wrong, marred beliefs. Rey's words helped me take a first step toward cutting the bonds of legalism and a works mentality—untruths that had followed me even into a saving faith in God. Rey listened to God, looked deeply into my heart, and saw a girl whose beliefs

> *"If everything goes wrong, will you make it? Will your faith survive?"*

about God had gotten off track and had tangled her up. It's so easy for those of us who love perfection to get our perspectives of God skewed by our hidden core beliefs.

Instead of seeing God as loving and gracious, we see Him as a taskmaster. Instead of knowing He loves us lavishly, we think He bestows love in measure with our output. Our subtle shift to wrong beliefs leaves us exhausted, disillusioned, and shut down. Those wrong beliefs need to be shattered before we can experience renewal.

Women who adhere to the Never Good Enough list also become

spiritually fatigued, and their relationship with God is damaged by believing they never can earn His love. Instead of believing that God's sacrifice of His Son is all we need, Never Good Enough Girls feel defeated by their own lack. Sins of the past stack up as witnesses to the "fact" that they'll never be able to enjoy God's love when they can't even love themselves. Accusing voices from childhood repeat, "You'll never amount to anything," or they tell themselves, "Your past has become your present," or some other crushing self-talk. Fear of future judgment is debilitating. For them, the race of life is already finished and lost. Even standing at the starting line, the Never Good Enough Girl has no hope in her heart. She creates a protective shell of outward perfection, and disconnecting from life and relationships feels like the only option. Though God lovingly beckons her to come into a life of freedom and peace, she turns away, feeling defeated before she even starts.

## CHOOSING *RELATIONSHIP* OVER *LISTS*

In the "Going Deeper" section for the previous chapter, I asked you to look at the story Jesus told about the rich young man. It's a particularly fascinating story as we think about the Good Girl List (or, in this case, the Good Guy List) and the Never Good Enough List. In just a few sentences we see the rich young man lay down one list and pick up the other.

> *As Jesus started on his way, a man ran up to him and fell on his knees before him. "Good teacher," he asked, "what must I do to inherit eternal life?" "Why do you call me good?" Jesus answered. "No one is good—except God alone. You know the commandments:*

*'Do not murder, do not commit adultery, do not steal, do not give*
*false testimony, do not defraud, honor your father and mother.'"*
*"Teacher," he declared, "all these I have kept since I was a boy."*

(Mark 10:17–20, NIV 1984)

Good girls, do you hear your own voice here? I sure do! Even while Jesus is telling us that the only one who is truly *good* is God, we— along with the young man—protest and tell Him that He's mistaken, because *we've* gotten it right. We believe in the redeeming power of our own checklist, and we blurt out our accomplishments despite Jesus' efforts at straightening our wonky point of view.

*Jesus looked at him and loved him. "One thing you lack," he said.*
*"Go, sell everything you have and give to the poor, and you will*
*have treasure in heaven. Then come, follow me."*

(Mark 10:21)

That first line, "Jesus looked at him and loved him," melts my heart every time. Instead of being disgusted by the young man's self-righteousness, which must have been stinking to high heaven, or disdainful of the young man's lack of understanding, Jesus *loves* him. What a simple, pure, and heartrending statement. Jesus saw him—the real him, the deepest him, the beyond-the-list him—and still loved him.

In the truest expression of love, Jesus' answer to the young man was an attempt to free him from his list of good deeds that could never make him truly good and grant him the eternal life he desired. The rich young man needed one thing to gain what he wanted: *relationship with Jesus.* So Jesus used the man's area of deepest struggle—

his dependence on riches—to expose the list that held him back from true riches. Giving up his wealth would have allowed him to enter into a vibrant relationship with Jesus.

In that moment, the young man had a choice. He could give up his wrong belief that his money and his righteous acts made him who he was; he could hand over the Good Guy List and give away his money for the one thing it couldn't buy—freedom; and he could choose relationship with God, the ultimate Provider of both righteousness and material essentials. But instead, the rich young man chose to hold on to his money, his list, and his wrong beliefs with the desperation of a drowning man clinging to an anchor.

> *At this the man's face fell. He went away sad, because he had great wealth.*
>
> (Mark 10:22)

By making this choice, he walked away from divine relationship with his pockets full and his heart empty. As Jesus said in Luke 12:21, "A person is a fool to store up earthly wealth but not have a rich relationship with God" (NLT). We each have the same choice that the rich young man had. Will we choose to align our beliefs with the truth or stay bound to the lists we've grown to love? Will we choose to see our pet beliefs as the captivity they truly are and turn to a relationship with God, selecting His way as the truth that sets us free?

> *The rich young man walked away from divine relationship with his pockets full and his heart empty.*

34

## ACTUALLY *RESTING* IN THE LOVE OF GOD

Months after my coffee date with Rey, I was still wrestling to let go of my lists and experience God's love. I felt like a student working on a PhD who was sent back to kindergarten, and I wasn't making any headway. "Why can't I feel the love of God?" I blurted out to Rey one day. "I've read books about it. I've listened to sermons about it. I've written about it. I've sung songs about it. I've thought and thought about it. I'm completely immersed, so why can't I get it? I'm working so hard!"

She let the silence sit for a beat before a big grin spread across her face. "Did you hear yourself?" she asked. "You can't *work* to know the love of God. You have to *rest* in the love of God." Then she encouraged me to relax and pray, asking God to reveal His lavish love to me in a deep, transforming way. I had no idea it would take a trip to India for me to get it.

Several months later at a women's conference in Kolkata, India, our team began an interactive exercise conceived by my creative teammate Nanette. She taught a session about becoming the bride of Christ, sharing her story of human heartbreak and Jesus' healing, and then she led us in a wedding simulation. Guiding the women to line up in two rows facing each other, Nanette pulled one woman aside, positioned her front and center at the end of the columns, and placed a veil on her head and a silk bouquet in her hands. "Close your eyes," Nanette directed. "Picture Jesus at the end of the aisle made by your friends. When you're ready, walk down the aisle to meet Jesus, your Bridegroom." One by one the women walked down the aisle as the "bridesmaids" lifted their hands over them and prayed, forming an arc of heaven-bound words.

Women were moved to tears as they participated in an activity that helped them join their hearts fully to Jesus. Just as I thought we were finished with this exquisite, emotional exercise, one of the leaders of the church walked over to a diminutive, wizened woman curled into near-invisibility in a chair on the periphery of the room. "It's your turn, Auntie," the leader said as she helped the skinny, weak woman to her feet. The wife of the local pastor began to whisper in my ear as the pair headed to the "wedding." "That woman is dying," she explained. "She's lived her whole life as a Hindu, but just two weeks ago, when I visited her home, she gave her heart to Jesus." At the end of the aisle, Nanette gently placed the veil on the woman's gray head and lowered the bouquet into her wrinkled hands. Tears poured down the old woman's face as she hobbled down the aisle.

Here was a woman who, for most of her life, had missed the love of God because of the fear and superstition of her native religion. He had always been there, loving, drawing, and wooing her heart until in the midst of her sickness and the pronouncement of her numbered days, she abandoned everything to take hold of His love. I watched as she walked feebly down an aisle toward Jesus, His love healing her of a lifetime of hurts and making her radiant and strong despite her fragile frame.

As I watched her weep, something broke inside me, and I found myself kneeling on the cold, concrete floor sobbing. God's love cracked through the hard shell around my heart and began to heal me of seeking a life *for* God instead of *with* God. The ever-present reality of God's love for me had never changed, but I had not soaked myself in it. I had walked into a place of self-sufficiency that left me with a weary hollowness, which only God's presence could fill.

Seeing a weak, impoverished old woman—who had little time left to give to God—fully surrendering to His love pierced my heart like a ray of sunshine piercing the fog. It's simple: He loves me—not because I have anything to give to Him, not because I live up to a powerless list, but simply because I'm His.

God doesn't call me to manufacture a feeling about Him. He simply calls me to pursue *Him*.

*Something broke inside me, and I found myself kneeling on the cold, concrete floor sobbing.*

After my experience in India, I stopped striving for perfect and started resting in the matchless, transformational work of Jesus on my behalf.

Each and every one of us can become the beautiful, loved Bride of Christ. Jesus stands waiting for us to join Him, with arms extended and love in His eyes. He invites each of us to let go of what we've held so tightly and experience the *wildness, fullness,* and *delight* of life with Him.

## Transformation Points

1. What things have you believed deep down about God that you know aren't true?

2. How have these beliefs kept you from a deeper relationship with God?

3. What steps will you take to study the Bible, God's truth about Himself, to know Him better and more truly?

### The Lie of Perfection

*I was created to produce perfection.*


### The Truth of God's Love

*Jesus produces perfection in me.*

*Chapter Two*

# DUST IN THE WIND

*Redefining the Truth of Who We Are*

"I think he's the one!" Through the phone, Becca's voice sizzled with excitement, and in my mind's eye, I could see her dancing eyes and sunburst smile. Even the purity of her heart came through in her words. "I think he's the one, Amy!" she repeated again.

But then Becca's voice fell as she explained her need. Years before, when her parents divorced, they settled on an unusual custody agreement. Becca lived with her mother while her brother lived with her father, and she rarely spent time with the males in her family. She and her mother had a good relationship, but there was a missing piece that made Becca's insecurities rise and her sense of urgency acute. "I have never seen married people interact, and now I'm thinking about marriage," she explained. "I need to see a normal Christian family. Can I hang out at your house?"

I gulped and then giggled. "I'm not promising anything *close* to normal, but you are always welcome."

Despite my disclaimer, preparations instantly began swirling through my mind. I started planning the most gourmet lunch my cuisine-challenged self can consistently pull off: a feast of grilled cheese, chips, and pickle spears. Then my mind turned to Scripture and the deep, ancient wisdom I needed to dispense to this girl I loved. During the days before our scheduled time, I cleaned every square inch of my house, including the corners of the shower in the bathroom upstairs. My offer to simply open my home and life faded away as my perfectionistic tendencies pulled me into a frenzy of unexamined activity. She didn't expect anything of me, but I expected lots of myself!

I pictured the scene between Becca and me before it even happened. The image I created was stunning. In it, my adoring husband returned from work with a kiss to the top of my beautifully coiffed head. My little boys were clean and well behaved. The house was a bastion of sparkling appliances, yummy fragrances, and peace, and I was the Christian June Cleaver, full of godly wisdom and a cheerful blessing to all. As I waited for our scheduled time, my foray into fantasy land didn't set off even one alarm in my self-deceived heart.

Our lunch together started fine. Becca played with Nolan, my then three-year-old, while I turned on the burners under the grilled cheese. Smiling, I returned to the kitchen table, where my Bible was opened to the passage I had been studying to share. So far, so good.

But toddlers tend to have plans of their own, and being out of the spotlight was not in Nolan's plan that day. His voice got louder and louder. When that didn't bring him back into the center of attention, he began climbing on me and nagging in his most piercing whine, "I wanna go outside, Mommy. Let's GO OUTSIDE, MOMMY!!"

Becca and I began by trying to ignore the un-ignorable. As his misbehavior and volume escalated, I tried my sweet kindergarten-teacher voice. "Now, Nolan, honey, Becca and I are trying to talk. Please go get some toys to play with, sweet potato sugar lump."

Nothing worked. As Nolan pitched a full-blown, head-spinning temper tantrum, I finally jumped up in exasperation, scooped up my flailing, shrieking child, and took him upstairs for a little . . . ahem . . . corrective conversation. Becca stared wide-eyed as I stormed from the room.

A short time later, I headed back downstairs to Becca with my hiccupping boy on my hip, grim determination set on my mouth and purpose in my step. Suddenly, I smelled it. I rushed back into my now smoke-filled kitchen, where Becca stood with full-moon eyes staring at the charred grilled cheese still resting on the glowing burner.

Time stopped while humiliation washed over me. As smoke swirled around my head and my seemingly demon-possessed spawn spun at my feet, I had a flash of brilliance. I knew exactly what to do. I looked over at the purse resting agape on my desk. I would simply hand Becca five dollars, explain it was for her lunch at McDonald's, and beg her to never, never, ever come back to my house again. Helping her escape this decidedly abnormal scene was clearly the only answer.

But then the One Whom I had forgotten but Who is always there spoke. Jesus whispered into my throbbing heart, "Amy, will you love Me enough and will you love her enough to open up your life—failures, flaws, and all?"

*Failures, flaws, and all, Lord?* I thought. *I'm not sure. I have a view of myself that's been violated here. I have an image I'm trying to build that's been thoroughly crushed right in front of a young, impressionable woman whom I wanted to think well of me. I think I just might be done with this project.*

## THAT SAME OLD PIT

It wasn't until later that I realized I had fallen into my old, self-dug pit again. I started with pure intentions. I wanted to help a girl I had come to love. My heart's desire was to give back to her in the way so many Jesus-placed women had poured their lives into me, and I was thrilled that it was my turn to lovingly serve Jesus by aiding one of His children.

Quickly, however, my heart went from the rest and peace of love into the high-gear grind of tasks. When tasks rise to the top of my priorities, I stop seeing myself as the richly loved daughter of King Jesus and start feeling like the stepdaughter dressed in rags scrubbing the floor under her Father's harsh, critical gaze. I start to see God as an unrecognizable taskmaster, and I begin to believe I'm only created to do His work.

Evidently, I'm not the only one. In a 2012 Barna survey[1], women were asked about their greatest struggles. Instead of identifying scripturally defined problems or sins such as lying, lust, or envy, 50 percent replied that their greatest struggle is disorganization, and 42 percent indicated inefficiency as their greatest difficulty. I think it's problematic and distressing that so many women describe their weakness in terms of productivity. Jesus gave His life to solve our greatest, death-producing problem—sin—but we perfectionists still focus on the work we think defines us. Viewing God simply as a divine project manager skews our

*Viewing God simply as a divine project manager skews our view of ourselves into dangerously prideful territory.*

view of ourselves into dangerously prideful territory, where the work of our hands is exalted above the work of God's Spirit. The path to the perfectionism pit is short when we trust our own methods and focus on our product.

It took a brand-new Christian, my friend Maggie, to set me straight on this years ago. Over dinner, I had been listening to Maggie talk excitedly about the work God was doing in her life. As a new believer, she was experiencing the transformation of her life with wide-eyed wonder. Everything about her new relationship with God was fascinating and fresh. She emanated joy.

Although I was enjoying Maggie's passion, I started to wonder, *Where did my joy go?* I could think of times when I had been consumed by watching and participating in the awesome work of God. I remembered mountaintop experiences when I felt full of passion, fire, and overwhelming joy. Yet here I was, many years Maggie's spiritual senior, and I was feeling exhausted and downright depleted. *How did I get to this place again?* I wondered. I was teaching Sunday school and speaking and writing with regularity. God had opened doors wide for ministry, but my batteries were running low.

At the end of our dinner together, Maggie and I exchanged prayer requests. She gave me a few, and then it was my turn. I struggled internally with how real I could be. Maggie was a new Christian. Surely I would discourage her if I confessed to a lack of joy and passion. God's still voice urged me to be transparent, though, and I found myself pouring out my heart in frustration. "I'm in God's Word every day as I prepare to teach," I explained to Maggie. "I'm always praying for the events and women where I'm going, but I feel wrung out and joyless. Please pray for me."

My sweet, wise friend gazed at me for a minute before she asked an essential question: "When was the last time that you spent time reading the Bible and praying when you weren't preparing for something? How long has it been since you just spent time with God to enjoy Him?"

Maggie had seen through all my spiritual rhetoric right to the source of the problem. I had been so busy talking to God—preparing, studying, delving, interceding, teaching, speaking—that I hadn't taken time to breathe in a deep breath of His Spirit. I hadn't taken time to worship God for Who He is, to meditate on a juicy piece of His Word, or to bask in His presence. In our drive to do all *for* "an audience of One," it's easy to neglect time *with* the One we love.

## A PERFECTIONIST'S MASCOT

A woman in the Bible had this same problem. Maybe because I identify with her so strongly, one of my pet peeves is how vilified she's been by women's ministries everywhere! Poor Martha. You probably know her story well, but please don't tune me out. She's the mascot for women everywhere who struggle with the pursuit of perfection, so let's take a fresh look. Luke 10:38–42 tells the short but powerful story:

> *As Jesus and his disciples were on their way, he came to a village where a woman named Martha opened her home to him. She had a sister called Mary, who sat at the Lord's feet listening to what he said. But Martha was distracted by all the preparations that had to be made. She came to him and asked, "Lord, don't you care that my sister has left me to do the work by myself? Tell her to help*

*me!" "Martha, Martha," the Lord answered, "you are worried and upset about many things, but only one thing is needed. Mary has chosen what is better, and it will not be taken away from her."*

Do you see Martha's natural wiring, her personality, coming out in this story? She's a woman with a gift of hospitality, a wonderful talent that's highly valued in Scripture, but somewhere along the way, her God-given gift and personality starts to drift toward the warped Good Girl Syndrome. Words like *distracted* and *preparations that had to be made,* as well as her demanding and highly sassy tone with Jesus, show that Martha had veered into an overdeveloped sense of responsibility. This detour led to strain in the relationships with both her sister and Jesus, the One she was working so hard to please. Sigh. I can so relate, and I'll bet you can see a little of yourself in the story too.

Recently, a friend who is a Messianic Jew revealed a new layer to me in this well-worn story. Martha definitely seems predisposed to ambition and perfection, the angle Americans constantly drive home, but she is actually functioning in the role determined for her by her gender, time frame, and culture. As American women, we're shocked by Martha's determination to be in the kitchen, but her contemporaries would have been astonished at Mary for being anywhere else but the kitchen.

Our beliefs about ourselves and our roles are keys to determining how we behave. Martha threw a hissy fit because she believed Mary belonged in the kitchen serving, and she couldn't envision herself or her sister anywhere else. I melt down when my idea of being a perfect mentor disappears like cheese on a hot burner. Because I define myself as a teacher, I prepare lessons during my time with God instead of simply enjoying Him.

Martha defined her identity by the roles she fulfilled—woman, sister, hostess. My default is to identify myself as wife, mother, keeper of my home, teacher, etc. I easily forget that I'm a *Daughter of the King*. Just like Martha, the moment I begin wearing my roles as my name rather than looking to the Name Above All Names for my identity, perfection lures me back into our dysfunctional romance.

What belief about yourself determines how *you* behave in negative ways? Do you define yourself as strong, so you feel trapped into being strong in every situation instead of asking for help? Do you believe you must be competent to be accepted, so you cover uncertainty or weakness at all cost? Do you think you need to be supermom, so you never apologize when you've failed?

We need to stop our madness, respond to His invitation to sit at His feet, and live out what we learn there. He confidently defines Himself, but He doesn't stop there. As our Creator, God defines each of us in ways that exceed our self-imposed limits and that set us free from negative labels. His definition of us transcends our beliefs about ourselves, which often lead us to negative outcomes.

*Our Creator defines each of us in ways that exceed our self-imposed limits and that set us free from negative labels.*

When we seek out what God says about us in Scripture, we gain a corrected perspective about who we become when we step into relationship with Him:

- We see ourselves as never measuring up, but God says we're a new creation (2 Corinthians 5:17).
- We see ourselves as unworthy, but He pours His grace upon us (Ephesians 2:8).
- We think we're ineffective, but God calls us salt and light (Matthew 5:13–14).
- We perceive our brokenness and struggle to earn love, but He says we're chosen, holy, and dearly loved (Colossians 3:12).
- We think we're just average, but God says we're His special possession (1 Peter 2:9).

Seeing ourselves in light of God, our relationship with Him, and His description of us in Scripture changes everything. Are we fatally flawed human beings? Do we fail to live up to others' expectations? Have we disappointed those we long to impress? Absolutely. But when we step into a surrendered relationship with Jesus, He redefines the truth of who we are in beautiful ways.

## TREASURED

Grasping God's truth about herself transforms a woman. I know it's true, because I saw it happen right before my eyes on the trip to India I mentioned earlier. Our little band of four women and one very brave man set off to lead two women's conferences. We packed light for our trip, but our hearts were full of prayers, messages, and plans grown over months of preparation.

Although we had dreamed big dreams, we couldn't imagine the

God-sized outcomes. We also couldn't imagine the size of the hurts needing to be healed or the damaging beliefs embedded in the shredded hearts of the women where we spoke. I am a woman who has been well loved in my journey through life, so I was astounded and grief-stricken by the stories told by my new Indian friends.

One woman returned late the second day of the conference bruised and cut by a beating with a fan blade. Her husband had been enraged because she attended a Christian conference.

A gifted young leader sobbed that her father told her he wished she were dead and would rather have a handicapped boy than a healthy, vibrant girl.

An exhausted, worn-down pastor's wife from Nepal confessed that she and her husband were preparing to leave the ministry because of the extreme persecution and isolation they faced.

A beautiful teenage orphan, solely supporting her grandmother and sister, returned home one evening from work to the announcement of her arranged marriage.

A grieving young woman related that after she was converted, her family members brushed by her in silence as if she didn't exist.

The stories of women with scars on their bodies and wounds on their hearts went on and on and on, so our team passionately poured the truth into these hurting women. "You are treasured by God. You are created in His image. You are completely loved by God. He could never love you any more or any less. He desires you so much that He calls you His own bride. Because you are His, He has a calling and a purpose for your life. You are God's treasure."

Slowly but surely, the tears of sorrow transformed into sobs of joy.

Understanding began to light the faces around us, and confessions of God's goodness abounded by the end of the conference.

The beaten woman not only bravely returned, she came back a third day with her precious son so he could also hear that he is God's treasure.

The young leader cried through praise and worship, knowing she was cherished by God and the women surrounding her.

The renewed pastor's wife testified she was excited to return and teach the women in her town.

The engaged teenager declared she would face marriage to a stranger, knowing that Jesus is her true husband.

The "invisible" woman prayed that she would be Jesus' love to her parents and brothers.

At the end, one attendee approached my teammate Peggy. She looked Peggy in the eyes and said, "Thank you for making us important." Peggy quickly replied, "Honey, *God* made you important," to which the woman answered, "But we didn't know."

*Peggy quickly replied, "Honey, God made you important," to which the woman answered, "But we didn't know."*

## STEPPING INTO THE TRUTH ABOUT ME

When we embrace God's truth about ourselves and adopt His beliefs about us, we're able to take the first step toward change and healing. Asking God to show us our blind spots, heal our gaping wounds, and reveal our sins in our perfectionistic tendencies or overachieving hearts is the essential starting place for unmasking the glory of God's image in each of us. The truth about each one of us has been there all along. We just have to step into it.

I can almost hear Jesus whispering the same message he spoke to Martha to you and me: "Daughter," He says, "you are filled with a craving for others' approval. I invite you to experience the amazing life I've designed for you by seeking My approval alone." Or maybe, "That knot in your stomach is keeping you from taking the risk I've asked of you. Just jump! I promise to catch you! The first step takes faith, but the destination is pure joy."

When we join with Him by recognizing our faults and short-comings, agreeing with Him about them, and stepping into new choices of growth and learning, we begin to be free of constricting beliefs about ourselves. We start to balance conscientiousness with caring. Labor with love. Scheduling with straightened priorities. And we gain the soul-filling relationships we've been working so hard for and craving all along. Maybe best of all, we begin to strengthen our inner relationship with ourselves by becoming the women God dreamed of since before our birth.

## DUST WOMEN FOREVER

God, our compassionate and gracious Father, gently looks down on us and says, "I know how you are formed. I remember you are dust." And then He draws us to Scripture, His very words, to focus us on His eternal work instead of on our very temporal callings. Psalm 103 is a beautiful example of Scripture that reminds us of who we are within God's framework. I'm just going to quote a section, but I encourage you to open your Bible right now and read the whole thing. Don't worry. I'll wait for you!

> Praise the LORD, my soul;
> all my inmost being, praise his holy name.
> Praise the LORD, my soul,
>     and forget not all his benefits—
> who forgives all your sins
>     and heals all your diseases,
> who redeems your life from the pit
> and crowns you with love and compassion,
>     who satisfies your desires with good things
> so that your youth is renewed like the eagle's. . . .
> As a father has compassion on his children,
>     so the LORD has compassion on those who fear him;
> for he knows how we are formed,
>     he remembers that we are dust.
>
> (Psalm 103:1–5, 13–14)

He knows we are just dust—frail, fallen, and swept away by any gusting breeze. The realization that God is Lord, Forgiver, Healer, Redeemer, and King, while we are dust or grass and flowers that flourish, fade, and die, should not discourage us or make us despair in being small. On the contrary, we see all the good God pours out on us in our feeble state! He gives us forgiveness, healing (verse 3), redemption, love, and compassion (verse 4). He's slow to anger, pouring out grace instead, and He shows mercy instead of constantly holding our feet to the fire, which is exactly what we deserve. But He's not finished yet. As well as supplying our *needs*, He even lavishes us with good things that satisfy our *desires* (verse 5).

Louie Giglio rejoices this way in his excellent book *I Am Not but I Know I AM*:

> *The truth is, feeling small may not be so bad if in recognizing our smallness we come to realize the wonder of God—a God who is beyond our ability to fully describe or imagine, yet someone we are privileged to know, love, and embrace. Looking up from our tiny estate we are faced with the supremacy of a God who not only is fully capable of running the entire cosmos today—a task that doesn't tax Him in the slightest—but of sustaining the affairs of our lives as well.*[2]

Seeing ourselves as small in comparison to God's greatness isn't a place to wrestle. It's a place to rest. I can release my expectations of myself and how I live up to the expectations of others when I know that my loving, compassionate God is the only One I need to please. Rather than working to create my own perfection, I can trust the perfecting of my soul to Him. I won't lie and say His process is painless, but it's a route filled with peace and God's provision rather than the never-ending treadmill run of trying to do it myself. Seeing ourselves correctly as both loved and sinful is key to ending our love affair with Perfect.

> *Seeing ourselves as both loved and sinful is key to ending our love affair with Perfect.*

## KNOCKING OFF THE CHRISTIAN JUNE CLEAVER

Years ago, I stood in my smoke-filled kitchen with a naughty toddler, a precious but slightly afraid young woman, and a decision to make. Would I cling to my hand-carved view of myself—a woman who wanted to present the perfect image of herself and her family? Or would I surrender to my perfect Jesus—the One who was asking me to own my flaws and trust His sufficiency? Was I willing to be in an authentic relationship with Becca—a woman who needed to see a real marriage, not a plastic one?

Jesus whispered again, "Amy, will you love *Me* enough, and will you love *her* enough, to open up your life, failures, flaws, and all?" I don't always choose correctly, but that day I made the right decision and took a huge step toward breaking up with Perfect. I chose the woman God created me to be over the one I was fashioning with my own hands. I took a deep breath, turned to Becca, and said, "So much for the perfect Christian woman! Let's start a new batch of grilled cheese."

## Transformation Points

1. What role have you adopted as your identity?

2. How does seeing God correctly as loving and compassionate help you to see yourself better?

3. In what ways does knowing you are treasured allow you to give up your pursuit of perfection?

*The Lie of Perfection*

*My imperfections are the fault of others.*

*The Truth of God's Love*

*Only when I choose to be nothing
will I find my everything.*

## Chapter Three

# IT'S NOT YOU, IT'S ME

### *Choosing Relationships over Blame*

I called my friend with a plan for fun with our group, and as far as I was concerned, it was a well-thought-out, ideal plan. You already know how I love perfection, so heaven help the woman who gets in the way of my perfect plan. Oh dear.

From the very start of the conversation, it was like we were speaking two different languages. We couldn't seem to understand each other at all. I began with the assumption that she'd totally love my brilliant plan. I would explain it to her. She would love it. End of story. But she didn't love it. At. All. Suddenly emotions rose, battle lines were drawn, and wounds were inflicted. How did we get here?

I was positive *I* wasn't the problem. I had placed the call with good intentions. Hmph! My taking offense to her resistant attitude was totally justified. In fact, it was clearly her fault that this whole episode had exploded! . . . And just like that, the girl with an overdeveloped sense of responsibility abdicated ownership of any guilt. If you get in the way of my perfection, I'm absolved, you see.

Although I was firmly seated on my trusty high horse as we ended the conversation, a nagging feeling of unease lingered after we hung up. I wrestled with my thoughts over a little cooling-off period and then called a wise, truth-telling friend to either comfort me or correct me. I told her the basic outline of the conversation, trying to keep it neutral. Finally I asked her, "What do you think went wrong?" She astutely turned the question back to me: "What could you have done differently?"

Me? Why would she ask such a question? It clearly wasn't my fault. At first I couldn't dredge up one thing I could have done differently; but after some reflection, God began to whisper to my heart. I saw the big mistakes I'd made. I had called my friend during an extremely busy time in her life with a suggestion that would add to her workload. Instead of being sensitive, I pushed and pushed my own agenda. As she held her ground, my defensiveness increased, making my responses sharp and prickly.

My friend gently prodded: "How could you have listened more carefully? Would truly listening have made you more compassionate? How could you have responded with more grace?"

Those questions pierced my heart, because suddenly I could see my part in the conflict with clarity. It wasn't my friend who was the stumbling block. My pride over the plan I created made my ego rise up large and out of proportion to the problem. Justifying my own vehemence was easy because I was so sure I was right. I put my plans above her needs, and I was quick to blame her when our agendas conflicted.

I wish I could say this was a one-time deal, but when I reflected back on the full-blown conflicts I'd engaged in, I could see a repeated attitude. Because I follow a Good Girl List, most of the time I do "nice" pretty well, but there's no wrath like that of a perfectionist scorned. Maybe if you adhere to the Never Good Enough List, your reaction would be different. You might not feel confident enough to stand up for your idea, so you wouldn't fight at all. You'd just hang up the phone . . . and simmer. Resentment would lodge like a stone in your heart toward your friend who messed with your perfect plan.

Either way—expressed anger or silent resentment—perfectionists tend to be blamers, and along with that *blame* comes *comparison* and *covetousness*. Whichever of these three we dabble in, we perfectionists often see others as obstacles to what we want rather than people we are in relationship with. We've talked about how perfection can skew our view of God and ourselves, but it can also distort our view of others—our family, friends, children, husbands, or coworkers.

In spite of my story above, I don't frequently struggle with blame when it comes to my friends, but my marriage is a different story. One particular blame issue plagued my marriage for far too long. For years I held up my parents' marriage as the closest to perfect I had seen. They rarely argued, and they had a routine I grew up admiring as idyllic. At night they went to bed together, and in the morning they rose together. As their feet simultaneously hit the floor, they would begin to make the bed together, one on each side, while they quietly talked and greeted the morning. I absorbed this utopia as a girl and walked down the aisle with it embedded in my bride's heart.

> *We perfectionists often see others as obstacles to what we want rather than people we are in relationship with.*

From our first day at home together after the honeymoon, I started a pattern of blame, comparison, and covetousness that plagued my marriage for years. I'm a morning person, but Barry is a night owl. Not only does he not care about the bed being made (while I'm absolutely addicted to the perfect feeling of slipping your feet into smooth sheets at night), he is too bleary in the morning to care for either conversation or feet meeting the floor in synchronization. He prefers the snooze button and a cup of coffee before any words or activity.

And so I *blamed* Barry for not cooperating with my plan for the perfect marriage, I *compared* our morning routine (or lack of routine) to my parents' bliss, and I was *covetous* of the perfect marriage my parents had.

Only recently did I confess to Barry that for more than fifteen years I clung to my hyped-up mental picture of perfection, scorned his uniqueness, and blamed him for our marriage not reaching its full potential. He was shocked, because for all those years, I had kept my perfect picture locked in my head, never telling him of my petty unhappiness.

When I talked to my mother about their morning routine, she laughed out loud at the notion that their bed-making schedule was a key to their happy marriage. Her reaction, combined with my husband's, revealed how crazy I'd been to hang on to this ideal picture. It existed *only* in my head. My mother, who was part of this picture, pointed out that what I wanted to bring into my own reality wasn't even *real*. I had pinned my dreams of a flawless marriage on a symbol I created. Yes, my parents make the bed together, but their relationship isn't perfect. They simply have different issues than Barry and I. Instead of embracing our new patterns as a unique couple, I blamed Barry, flooding our relationship with an underlying current of discontent.

How had I let getting the bed made affect the way I viewed my whole marriage for almost two decades? Why had I reacted so harshly toward my friend over her objections to my "perfect plan"? I now see those reactions as ridiculously overblown, but at the time they made complete sense. As I pursued the perfect pictures in my head, my perspective got twisted. I didn't set out to diminish the people involved in the problems, but I did. What I thought would help all involved actually caused great hurt to the relationships.

## MY PIECE OF THE PIE

I have a sneaking suspicion I might not be the only one who has fallen into this trap. Perfectionists are professionals when it comes to the blame game. The picture of our perfectly scheduled day at work collapses when a coworker interrupts with a crisis. Our perfect vacation is ruined when the friends along for the ride suggest a different itinerary for the day. The carefully planned women's event is considered a flop when team members don't decorate to our specifications. Everything was perfect until *he/she/they* came along.

It's easier to blame others than to take a hard look at difficult truths about ourselves. Often, we perfectionists cause great harm by clinging to carefully constructed images rather than embracing our beautifully flawed realities. Another term for "carefully constructed images" could be "unrealistic expectations." In *The Best Yes*, Lysa Ter-Keurst warns us of the danger of overblown anticipation: "Unrealistic expectations become unmet expectations. And unmet expectations are like kindling wood—it only takes but a spark of frustration to set them ablaze and burn those involved."[1]

Anytime we assess the angst we're feeling over a less-than-perfect circumstance as someone else's fault, we have probably gotten off track. It can happen before we've even realized the lie is creeping into our heads to make its home. Blame whines, "We'd have a better marriage if only he'd do it my way." Comparison whimpers, "You're not as talented as her, so you'll never have the life you really want." Covetousness hisses, "If I only lived in that neighborhood, I'd be part of the 'in' crowd too." Steadily, resentment grows toward those we're measuring ourselves against, all because we're holding our pictures of perfection more tightly than the people we love. Relationships shatter when we value perfection over people.

Recently a friend pointed out the wrong belief that lies in the center of blame, comparison, and covetousness. It's the belief that all resources—time, talents, opportunities, wealth, love, etc.—are like a pie. Instead of knowing God as the all-sufficient, infinite Supplier of these precious commodities, we see the pie as limited and only divisible between so many people. That core belief and fear of being left out leads us to scramble and grab for our piece of the pie. We want our slice all to ourselves and right now! It's the front-runner to thoughts like, *If I didn't have to meet the needs of these kids, I could follow my dreams.* In that scenario, you blame the kids for getting the majority of the time pie while you are left wanting. Or maybe you've thought, *If I had the contacts she has, I'd be successful too.* In comparing yourself to another, you decide that someone else has an unfair advantage over you. If only you had a bigger piece of the influence pie, you'd achieve what you want. Or maybe you see someone who appears to have exactly what you want and you fall into the trap of coveting her gifts. For each situation, we hold tightly to a picture of perfection, thinking that just a little more would complete the picture . . . more time, more contacts, more ability, more attention, or more bed-making. In this view, self is the center and others are obstacles.

## ON THE PATH TO PERFECTED

Our humble Jesus presents a counterintuitive solution to our acute feeling of needing more to measure up. As Jesus often does, He turns our expectations of how the world works on its head. Through Paul, Jesus gives the church at Philippi a lesson that speaks directly to the blaming, comparing, covetous heart of a perfectionist. Philippians 2:5–11 is a massive load of truth, so let's read it as a whole and then unpack the pieces.

*In your relationships with one another, have the same mind-set as Christ Jesus:*

> *Who, being in very nature God,*
>     *did not consider equality with God*
>     *something to be used to his own advantage*
> *rather, he made himself nothing*
>     *by taking the very nature of a servant,*
>     *being made in human likeness.*
> *And being found in appearance as a man,*
>     *he humbled himself*
>     *by becoming obedient to death—*
>     *even death on a cross!*
> *Therefore God exalted him to the highest place*
>     *and gave him the name that is above every name,*

> *that at the name of Jesus every knee should bow,*
> *in heaven and on earth and under the earth,*
> *and every tongue acknowledge that Jesus Christ is Lord,*
> *to the glory of God the Father.*

Here we go! Let's take this one little bite at a time.

*In your relationships with one another, have the same mind-set as Christ Jesus.*

Relationship is the forge where Jesus refines His followers. Although God has wired us to move into relationship, I've found it's a most difficult place to make permanent residence. It's messy, painful, and ever changing. If we submit ourselves to God's work in relationships, taking on Jesus' mind-set, it's where the blaming heart learns personal accountability. It's where comparisons become insignificant. It's where the covetous heart learns contentment. In our relationships, we're called to give up our own way of thinking, our flawed beliefs, and to adopt Jesus' divine thoughts as the higher way. The next verses show us just how astounding Jesus' thoughts and values are.

*Who, being in very nature God, did not consider equality with God something to be used to his own advantage . . .*

In some digging, I found this definition of the word *nature* in this verse: "The nature or character of something, with emphasis upon both the internal and external form."[2] Jesus is literally God inside and out. Even as I type, my mind cannot expand around this thought. Fully God.

Fully man. Jesus, Immanuel, God with us. Whole books have been written on this topic by much smarter people than me, so I wrap my feeble mind around it with some simple but profound truths. Jesus is everything. He is Creator. He is King. He is Lord. As God, He resides in heaven, a place more perfect than any perfectionist can imagine. His position is eternally established no matter His location. And then . . .

*he made himself nothing by taking the very nature of a servant, being made in human likeness.*

Rather than trading on His rightful position, Jesus intentionally gave up the perfection of heaven and chose a new position. "He made himself nothing." He isn't nothing, but He *chose* to become nothing. Although He holds power and authority and is due respect, He elected to abdicate the rights and benefits of His high status by giving up the privileges He rightfully holds with His rank. Giving up perfection, He accepted an assignment in a flawed, broken, sinful world as a servant.

*And being found in appearance as a man, he humbled himself by becoming obedient to death—even death on a cross!*

Why did Jesus give up the true perfection of His rightful home? Because He values relationship more. He loves His Father endlessly, and He loves us lavishly. From the time relationship was broken between man and God by sin, the Father's plan always contained the sting of death. Jesus' death bought unhampered relationship with Jesus for you and me, and this relationship with us brings Him great joy. The beauty of the following piece of Isaiah 53:11 moves my heart every time: "After he has suffered, he will see the light of life and be satisfied." Jesus gave up the perfection of heaven to have the satisfaction of a relationship with you and me.

I'm wrecked to see God's view of true perfection and then compare it to my own warped view. In His economy,

> *In God's economy, simple obedience to His direction is the path to perfection.*

and in contrast to my complex pictures of perfection, simple obedience to His direction is the path to perfection. We often use the term *love language* when we want to talk about how we show love to someone. God's love language is obedience. Obedience communicates our love for God, and it gives Him pleasure.

When Jesus was baptized out of obedience to His Father in Matthew 3, God's response was a beautiful affirmation of the perfection of obedience: "This is my Son, whom I love; with him I am well pleased" (Matthew 3:17). We hear echoes of these affirming words in our promised reward as obedient children: "Well done, good and faithful servant!" (Matthew 25:21). Doesn't reading it make you long to hear it?

I recently heard Christine Caine speak, and she pointed to this truth: *obedience rather than works is the route to God's pleasure.* She maintained that the rewarding words "Well done, good and faithful servant!" are applied equally to the woman who devotedly leads a small weekly Bible study in her living room and the woman who authors a *New York Times* bestseller, speaks in coliseums, and leads thousands to Christ. Both women are considered righteous and perfected in their Father's eyes because of their obedience.

One piece of the pie isn't superior to the other; rather, obedience is the great equalizer. Jesus leads the way in showing us the perfecting power of obedience. By bringing obedience into a flawed world, He brought beauty into imperfection. We can do the same when we bring our obedience to imperfect circumstances in our relationships.

*Therefore God exalted him to the highest place and gave him the name that is above every name, that at the name of Jesus every knee should bow, in heaven and on earth and under the earth, and every tongue acknowledge that Jesus Christ is Lord, to the glory of God the Father.*

Because Jesus valued relationship above perfection . . . because Jesus was everything but chose to become nothing . . . because Jesus subjected himself to death out of obedience, God not only restored Jesus to the perfection of heaven but exalted Him as the name above every name. God doesn't work within the confines of our piece-of-the-pie mentality. He works in the limitlessness of Kingdom generosity. We too find abundance in walking in the steps of Jesus.

Here's how I've wrapped my brain around this mind-blowing scripture:

- Jesus temporarily laid aside His eternal position of Lord to move into His chosen position of servant.
- Because His fully obedient life ended in death on the cross, He gained the earned position of Savior.
- Finally, the Father exalted Him further by giving Him the position of Lord.

Seeing this circle is life-changing. Jesus always has been and always will be Lord and Master of all, but because He chose humility, servanthood, and death, He was exalted by God to the position created for Him before time began.

The same principle applies to us in our Christian walk. Only when we choose humility, servanthood, and death-to-self like Jesus did can we truly step into becoming the person we were created to be since God wove us together. Jesus presents *choosing nothing* rather than *getting more* as the path to perfection. He shows us what "nothing" looks like—letting love cover a multitude of sins, choosing to give up our right to be right, dispensing life-giving words, and considering others above ourselves. We will only choose these virtues if we value relationship more than our own flawed view of perfection. Stepping into a chosen position of nothing gives us everything in return.

*Stepping into a chosen position of nothing gives us everything in return.*

As we look at the Philippians 2 passage, we see that the progression of Jesus' life went like this:

- Jesus gave up the true perfection of heaven. We're only called to give up the unreal picture of perfection living in our heads.
- Jesus chose to be a servant when He was actually Lord. We receive the amazing gift of serving the King of Kings and His people.
- Jesus died a physical death to purchase our salvation. We die to self to gain His salvation.
- God exalts humble Jesus above all. We are lifted into the most beautiful, truest version of who we are as we humble ourselves.

## NEAR MISS

The progression of my ministry life didn't start out on the obedient path that Jesus took. In fact, because of my covetousness, I almost killed my calling. Soon after accepting a leadership position in the women's ministry of my church, a friend on the team came up to me. "Oh! We forgot to tell you," she said with a grin. "You're in charge of the annual women's conference."

Despite the ambush (I mean surprise), I loved every minute of organizing the event. But as I interacted with our guest speaker, envy began to wind itself around my heart. If it could have spoken aloud, it would have said, "I want *that!*" I wanted her platform. I wanted her eloquence. I wanted her audience. I wanted her cute outfit.

I wanted her piece of pie.

Fortunately, I soon recognized these "wants" as signs of covetousness rather than signs of my calling. I knew God had called me to be the women's ministry director during that season—not to speak. Each time I desired what that speaker had, it took my focus off what God had for me—His truly perfect, gradually unfolding plan for my life. So I asked God to kill the weed of envy that was choking the breath from my calling to lead women. I asked Him to purify my motives and steer my heart to the women He had called me to serve. Because God faithfully shepherds our hearts when we let Him in, those desires steeped in bad motives ebbed away.

Several years later, in my quiet times with God, I thought I started to hear His whispers to me about a speaking ministry. My first reaction was to think, *There's that old, nasty envy again. God, purify my heart!* But this time was different. As I unpacked my motives and expectations, I realized God had changed me. Instead of thinking, *How can I get what she has?* I thought, *I only want what God has planned for me.* Instead of feeling jealousy toward anyone who had something I thought I might want, I rejoiced in how God was using others' gifts.

God had graciously refined my motives to just one, and that was to obey Him—seeking His perfect plan and calling, rather than sinking into a covetous desire for my own picture of perfection. This time stepping into speaking was a step of obedience; it was a move toward becoming all God had created me to be instead of seeing someone else as an obstacle to that dream.

It's so easy to let our own idea of the perfect life reign in our hearts. Maybe speaking isn't something you find pleasurable, let alone aspire to, but maybe you're the mom who dresses her children to impress others. Or maybe you're the employee who takes charge of the room to show your boss your readiness for the next step up.

There's nothing wrong with cute children or promotions, but so many times our underlying motives trip us up. Instead of being pure, they get mixed with negative motives that sully the outcome. We yell at our children for soiling those cute clothes on the playground. We subtly sabotage the coworker who got the promotion we're sure we deserved. In pursuing perfection, we run over people, oblivious to their feelings or needs. We feed resentment caused by blame, comparison, and covetousness. We miss the exquisite nature of our true selves because we're too busy building on the shaky foundation of unrealistic expectations.

## THE SELF-EXAMINATION ROOM

Looking at my motives with a magnifying glass has helped me curb my pie-in-the-sky syndrome. When I got super-honest with myself about the conflict with my friend at the beginning of the chapter, my level of offense revealed my heart. My feathers had gotten ruffled because I loved my *plan* more than the *people* the plan was designed to serve. The conflict was exacerbated by my perfectionism and my tendency to be hypersensitive to any pushback. Owning my part helped me to ask my friend for forgiveness for my insensitivity. We shared a good ending, with full relationship restoration, and I was able to live out Paul's admonition that precedes Philippians 2:5–11.

In Philippians 2:3–4, Paul commands, "Do nothing out of selfish ambition or vain conceit. Rather, in humility value others above yourselves, not looking to your own interests but each of you to the interests of the others." When I let go of the selfishness and conceit of my perfect ideal, I was able to wholeheartedly feel the needs of my friend and consider them above my own. When we put others first, pictures of perfection fade away and common ground emerges.

## PLAYING OUR POSITION

God's call to our hearts may seem counterintuitive. For God wants our hearts to focus on becoming *nothing*. Aiming for *nothing* does not reflect our status or worth—we are always holy and dearly loved children of the King. But *nothing* is to be our chosen position as a servant, imitating Jesus in His sacrifice of self. We always have a choice. We can choose a pie mentality or a Kingdom generosity. We must ask ourselves, "Is this a decision to get more or to choose nothing?" When we choose correctly, we step out of our view of perfection into a position of humility where we begin to look more like Jesus inside and out.

My husband is modeling this choice to humbly be like Jesus in a way that tickles the recesses of my neat-girl heart. Just yesterday, my husband returned from a business trip. That night he went to bed with me, and the next morning I heard his feet hit the floor in tandem with my own. He stood, winked, and said, "I missed you while I was gone. Let's make the bed together."

*Nothing is to be our chosen position as a servant, imitating Jesus in His sacrifice of self.*

I grinned from ear to ear as we worked together that morning, but that's not the best part. As we went our separate ways moments later, I realized that I no longer expected or required Barry to mold into my ideal image. Our relationship is far from perfect, but it's free from discontent. I don't see him as an obstacle to our growth. Jesus helped me break up with those expectations years ago. Although it was sweet to have a partner smoothing the sheets with me, it was much sweeter to know the door had been slammed right in Perfect's face.

## Transformation Points

1. Who has recently gotten in the way of your Perfect?

2. What was your reaction to that person?

3. How could choosing to be nothing change the situation? Do you need to make things right today?

*Part Two*

# BREAKING UP WITH
# SKEWED VALUES

*Getting Free from What Crowds Our Hearts*

*The Lie of Perfection*

*I can create the perfect image of me.*


*The Truth of God's Love*

*I am only perfect as I allow God to complete me.*

*Chapter Four*

# PAPER DOLL

*Breaking Our Shape-Shifting Cycles*

As a little girl, I loved the delight of a paper doll. I haven't seen them in the stores lately, so maybe only women of a certain age remember them. If you're my age, this may be a trip down memory lane, but if you're a younger chickadee, here's how they worked. The whole set came in a book with the doll printed on cardstock along with pages of stylish paper fashions for her to wear. I'd flip through the pages delighting in each colorful outfit, and then I'd break out my scissors. Sticking my tongue out one side of my mouth and squinting with my eyes just so, I'd guide my scissors down the dotted line with all the precision my tiny hands could muster. Soon a doll with her thin pile of wardrobe and accessories would accumulate. One by one, I'd try little Polly Paper Doll's outfits on her, folding the tabs neatly around her edges to hold her dresses, PJs, and play clothes snugly in place.

Paper dolls were fun. For a little while. However, the problem with them was twofold. They were two-dimensional, and they were fragile. It only took a few minutes of play before my frustrations would start.

Because she was flat, I couldn't hold her in my arms without her slipping out, and I couldn't stand her up without her falling down. She didn't have the substance to stand up to real-life activities like my cuddly baby dolls. After just a few rounds of playing dress-up and tea party, my dolly's paper tabs would rip off from the constant folding, and her now-worn body would begin to flop. Paper dolls are literally only the image of a real doll, and that was the root of the problem.

## THE IMAGE MACHINE

Our culture is obsessed with image. Hollywood, television, and every marketing ploy parade airbrushed images of the ideal life in front of us in a 24/7 news cycle. Social networking has amped up the image-making factory to a new high gear. Suddenly, we're able to present a self-shaped version of ourselves to whomever is watching. We take fifteen selfies and pick the best one to post, deleting all the ones that show our double chin. We can brag about a trip to a beautiful location without disclosing the amount of debt we accrued to get us there. We post accomplishments without telling of all the failures along the way. Here's the truth. I'm not proud of it, but I chose those examples because I've done every single one. I'm pretty sure I'm not the only one.

Let's take a look at some statistics about Facebook as one example. In 2008, Facebook had a whopping 100 million users; by the end of 2014, it boasted an unimaginable 1.4 billion.[1] The average Facebook user has about 130 friends[2] who let us in on everything from what they had for breakfast to the photos of their cat's last nap. Please don't get me wrong. I have two Facebook accounts, and I love the connection social networking brings. (Important note: I'll like the pictures of your cat napping if you'll like the pictures of my wiener dog peeking out from under her blanket!) I'm not being critical, but here are some additional stats that sat me back in my chair. In a recent survey, 21 percent of users confessed they checked Facebook in the middle of the night, and 34 percent said it was the first thing they do in the morning.[3]

Let's think about that. In the middle of the night, when our bodies naturally crave sleep, one out of five people feels compelled to check their friends' latest updates. Over one in three checks out the updates on their Facebook feed as soon as they wake up. Before they do anything else. Like brush their teeth. Or go potty. Now, let me tell you something. Because I'm a girl of a certain age with a certain amount of wear and tear on her bladder, I don't do *anything* before I go potty in the morning. However, you might catch me picking up my phone and checking my newsfeed just after that little emergency trip.

What is driving us to such obsessive behaviors? What do these statistics tell us? Although the study doesn't give the cause, I believe it's an obsession with measuring ourselves against others, and I'm not exempt from the madness. Good Girls and Never Good Enough Girls alike fall into the trap of trying to shape how others see us. It makes me sad to reflect on how often I've lived a paper-doll life, trying to create an image of myself to impress others and gain acceptance rather than living the purest version of the woman God created me to be. I cringe over all the times I've scanned the room or studied social media trying to fig-

> *For years, I lived a paper-doll life, trying to create an image of myself to impress others and gain acceptance.*

ure out how I can do it all better. It's a disastrous recipe for never feeling good enough and adopting a cookie-cutter mentality.

Why do Good Girls and Never Good Enough Girls have this tendency to shape our own image? It goes right back to that craving for relationships. "If I appear all together, she'll like me." "If I look this way, maybe he'll ask me out, and it will be true love at last." "If I do my quiet time, prayers, and service projects right, I'll be closer to God." These are the kind of underlying thoughts that are the catalyst for laboring over our image creation.

I've done it myself over and over again. I remember rereading some old letters I wrote to our church's women's ministry team members and hearing my mentor's voice instead of my own. She was a godly woman I admired, but instead of just learning from her, I had stepped into her image, hoping I too would earn the label "godly woman." In my freer high school days, I was known for my funky personal style, which got a little wacky at times. In my thirties—the prime time of my image-building struggles—I toned down to blandness, trying to create the image of respectable wife and mother.

Snip by snip we perfectionists cut the outline of a cardboard image with a perma-smile and fragile paper coverings to fit the rage of the moment. But there's a deep flaw in that way of living. God never meant for us to create our own image. He made us to bear His. In Genesis 1, the stunning passage revealing creation, God does something unique and amazing in His creation of men and women.

*Then God said, "Let us make mankind in our image, in our likeness,*
*so that they may rule over the fish in the sea and the birds in the sky,*
*over the livestock and all the wild animals, and over all the crea-*

*tures that move along the ground." So God created mankind in his own image, in the image of God he created them; male and female he created them. God blessed them and said to them, "Be fruitful and increase in number; fill the earth and subdue it. Rule over the fish in the sea and the birds in the sky and over every living creature that moves on the ground." Then God said, "I give you every seed-bearing plant on the face of the whole earth and every tree that has fruit with seed in it. They will be yours for food. And to all the beasts of the earth and all the birds in the sky and all the creatures that move along the ground—everything that has the breath of life in it—I give every green plant for food." And it was so.*

*God saw all that he had made, and it was very good.*

(Genesis 1:26–31)

One of the beauties of bearing the image of the One True God is our individuality. He lovingly creates each image bearer with her own diversity and uniqueness. He's not a cookie-cutter kind of God. He's the God who created over seventeen thousand colorful, fluttering species of butterflies when a utilitarian god would have created a single pollinator. If we'll bear God's image instead of trying to create our own, we can live in the abundance of the passage above. God uses His image in our lives to deliver a breathtaking variety of personalities, heart-nourishing love, satisfying work, and rich provision. The problem with shaping our own image rather than being God's image bearer is that our own images are two-dimensional—not reflecting the whole of who we are—and

> *God never meant for us to create our own image.*

they're fragile, liable to fall down like a house of cards the moment one piece of the image fails.

## THE SHAPE-SHIFTER

Creating an image of perfection is a never-ending, exhausting activity because the measure of perfection keeps shifting, depending on which crowd serves as our current measuring stick. The perfect sorority girl tries to live up to a very different image than the perfect athlete. The perfect socialite works to have an image that is in stark contrast to the perfect revolutionary. The perfect preppy disdains the perfect punk. Not only do these personas divide women instead of creating relationship and community, these perfect images start a cycle of never-ending shape-shifting.

I suffered most from shape-shifting when I had my first baby. My friends loaded me up with their recommended parenting books, and being a voracious reader, I dug right into them. Soon, I envisioned two supermoms in my mind. The first was Earth Mama Mom. She wore a bohemian skirt, chandelier earrings, and a quilted baby sling as her predominant and most important accessory. Earth Mama Mom cheerfully flexed with her baby's every need, cuddling up with her in the family bed at night or confidently supplying her a source of nourishment at a moment's notice no matter where they were—home, a restaurant, or in the middle of Macy's.

Then there was supermom number two, Right-on-Schedule Mom. This mom wore chinos and a dry-cleaned shirt that was always unwrinkled because she only picked up her baby when it was time—time for a meal, time for a nap, or playtime. Right-on-Schedule Mom's baby slept through the night at two weeks in her own snazzy crib and sat up before anyone else in their Mommy and Me group. Any natural "sources of nourishment" were tented in public and permanently covered at precisely one year, when they were replaced by a regular cup.

How to choose? How to choose? Each seemed perfect in its own way, and I vacillated between them. One day when I corrected Barry's fathering for the millionth time with, "The book says—" he interrupted with frustration, "Which book would that be?" With my brain spinning and my heart torn, I finally realized that I was trying to figure out the wrong thing. I didn't need to choose an ideal supermom, I needed to allow God to show me how to be the best mom to the baby He had given me. That realization was one tiny step toward mothering freedom and a giant step toward letting go of image.

During that same time of struggle, I went to a friend's wedding shower. I loved being with my teacher friends from the school where I taught before I left to stay home with my baby. We chatted endlessly, catching up on all the news from school, and I went on and on about a very part-time job I had gotten teaching for the local community college. All was well until in the silence of my car I realized that I had only talked about work. I hadn't shared anything about the joys of my highest priority, sweet little baby Anson.

As I reflected, my heart was broken at my obvious attempts to shape others' perceptions of myself. When I was with my friend group of stay-at-home moms, I rarely talked about my job because I feared their disapproval. But in the company of my former work friends, I didn't talk about anything except work in an attempt to shape an image of myself as a working woman who still fit in with them. Shape-shifting. Truth-bending. Working hard to create an image molded to the current crowd. My image was fragile, shifting with the prevailing winds and knocked down by anyone who knew the truth about me. Here's the reality of who I am: I've been a mostly stay-at-home mom who also loves to work. There. Is that so terrible? I'm learning not to be shaped by the fear of what others will think. Only when we lay down that fear can God shape us into bearers of His precious image.

## EMBRACING ANOTHER DIMENSION

Here's the huge difference between my idea of the perfect image and living in God's image. Creating an image is measuring up. Living in God's image is filling up. In truth, as Pascal suggested, we are dough-nut people created with a God-shaped hole, but God's best hope is for us to be *whole*. God wants us to be bursting with Him so that we go from flat paper dolls, hollow images we've created, to multidimen-sional creations full of every good gift He gives.

> *Creating an image is measuring up. Living in God's image is filling up.*

I've wrestled with the difference between my own efforts at creating an image and living the life God has created for me. I struggle with the fine lines between spiritual disciplines and legalism, good behavior and behavior that makes me look good, wise decisions and decisions I manipulate to appear wise. Since I've learned to lean on Scripture for infallible direction, I've turned there; but even Scripture confused me on this matter. I sought out a trusted friend with theologian-like knowledge to help me and exclaimed to her, "But the Bible *does* tell us to be per-fect! Right there in Matthew 5:48 Jesus says, 'Be perfect, therefore, as your heavenly Father is perfect.'" She just smiled and sent me home to do some studying and to look up the meaning of the word *perfect* in its context.

As the root meaning of the word flashed onto my computer screen, I sat in teary-eyed silence. The truer translation of the word *perfect* in this verse is to be "whole," "complete," or "mature." I may be mixed up about lots of things, but suddenly I had clarity on a big step toward breaking up with Perfect. God is calling us from the hollowness of self-made perfection to the wholeness of God-given completion. He is doing a perfecting work in us, longing to free us—day by day—from our false image of perfection, until we are living in the freedom, joy, and fullness of life for which we were created.

While our pursuit of perfection and a flawless image drains us of energy, God's work of perfecting fills us with peace. His perfecting entails spiritual disciplines—like study and prayer—as well as the rest of knowing His Spirit is sufficient to shape us. His perfecting opens our hearts to release our dearly loved views of good behavior and embraces God's ultimate good. It looks to Him for wisdom instead of subscribing to the standards of our current group. It trusts that God is big enough to turn even our flaws into something usable and to redeem the failures of our past.

## TARNISHED TO BLESSED

Recently, as my pastor wrapped up a study of the book of Ruth, I saw this reality of God's perfecting work in a beautiful blessing. You may know the Bible story of Ruth, but here's a quick recap. Naomi and Ruth found themselves alone in a man's world without their men.

Naomi, Ruth's mother-in-law, lost her husband and both her boys, including Ruth's husband, so they traveled back to Israel from the foreign land where they'd been living. When they arrived in Israel, God began a stunning redemption of their story. He provided physical provision and restoration of family through the marriage of Ruth to Boaz, and the couple produced a child who became a member of the lineage of Jesus. Here is the blessing found at the end of the story, given by the elders of the community over Ruth on the day of her marriage to Boaz:

> *Then the elders and all the people at the gate said, "We are witnesses.*
> *May the LORD make the woman who is coming into your home*
> *like Rachel and Leah, who together built up the family of Israel.*
> *May you have standing in Ephrathah and be famous in Bethle-*
> *hem. Through the offspring the LORD gives you by this woman,*
> *may your family be like that of Perez, whom Tamar bore to Judah."*

(Ruth 4:11–12)

The mention of the sisters Rachel and Leah in this passage takes my breath away. Rachel's story begins like a lovely fairy tale as she's romantically pursued by Jacob and becomes his wife. But when her sister-wife, Leah (also married to Jacob), became pregnant and gave Jacob multiple sons, Rachel grew desperate and gave her maidservant, Bilhah, to Jacob. Her plan was that Bilhah would bear a son on Rachel's behalf. Rachel was not exactly the bastion of good behavior and squeaky-clean image that you'd expect to be spoken over you when you're being blessed.

Then there's Leah—the less desirable, homely sister—who was

given in matrimony to the deceived and crestfallen Jacob in place of her sister, Rachel. After Jacob also married Rachel, creating a situation ripe for any reality TV producer, Leah seethed in competition with Rachel over Jacob's love, and when she developed infertility issues of her own, she too handed her maidservant over to Jacob. I've always had compassion for Leah, but as far as image goes, *pitiful* may be the kindest thing that can be said.

*I've always had compassion for Leah, but as far as image goes, pitiful may be the kindest thing that can be said.*

Next, we come to Tamar, who is the queen of cracked images. In Tamar's story, she is so desperate to conceive a child to continue the family line that she disguises herself as a prostitute in order to seduce her dead husband's father. Sit on that for just a second. This story icks me out every time I read it or think too deeply about the logistics. There are lots of lurid images and nasty names that come to mind if we just look at Tamar's story on the surface.

But God's assessment is diametrically opposed to our own. While we work to create an image that is primarily veneer, God is moving beneath the surface of our lives doing His perfecting, redeeming work. He is the image consultant who can be trusted to create an eternal reputation. In spite of Rachel and Leah's catfighting, God made them builders of a great nation. Tamar is not only remembered as the blessed mother of Perez but is given the highest honor of inclusion in the Messiah's lineage. These women's images were restored from tarnished to exemplary.

How can we begin to take steps to move out of our self-created image into God's pure image? How can we move toward putting our image entirely into God's trustworthy hands? We do so through a series of choices.

### Choose authenticity over masks.

When we create our own image, we begin to wear masks to cover our flaws. The trouble is, our masks disguise the glory of our truest God-created selves. The light within Jesus lovers is dimmed by the veil of masks. But every time we make a small choice to reveal our true selves instead of hiding behind a mask, we are making the choice to bear God's image instead of shaping our own.

Several years ago, I needed to wrestle off a mask and deal with humility. "I don't *want* to go bowling," I said, hearing a cringe-inducing whine creep into my voice.

My whole extended family was enthusiastically preparing for a fun outing, but I was dragging my feet. In reality, I don't dislike bowling *terribly*. The thing I really, really, *really* don't like is doing things I'm not good at. And I'm terrible at bowling.

Avoidance or quitting is my natural default. Why? Because "competent" is one of the labels I crave. Competency is a mask I love to slap on to cover my weaknesses.

This may seem like a really silly story to illustrate an important point, but it's one small choice that illustrates how doing things my way can interfere with the gifts God has in store for me. How many times have I missed out on deeper connection with someone because I've refused to take off my mask? Many, many times. Some of them I can remember, and because it's such a terrible habit, some I probably didn't even notice.

Next time, instead of whining, I'm determined to kick up my heels, bowl a few rounds, and giggle instead of wince at every ball that goes in the gutter. I'd rather be authentically bad at bowling with my family than appear competent all by myself!

### Choose God's Word over personal preferences.

In Amos 7, God reveals Himself and His Scripture as a plumb line. A plumb line is used in construction as a way to determine a true straight line, and God's Word serves that purpose in our lives. I'm finding that if I'll turn to His ancient truths to find my highest purpose, I can avoid chasing a flawed image based on current trends or beliefs. Scripture not only leads us in a straight line, it steers us to our best selves as we follow it closely.

Molding our own image takes painstaking strategy and exhausting work. But when we choose to follow God through living by Scripture, we are choosing to *abide* in Him rather than *strive* on our own. This choice also sets us apart. One of the girls in my Sunday school class shared a quote her father tossed at her each day as she left for school: "Be a thermostat, not a thermometer!" When we choose to let God set the standard, we also set an attractive standard for those around us, pointing directly back to Jesus. As our lives point to Jesus, we can confidently say with Paul, "Follow my example, as I follow the example of Christ" (1 Corinthians 11:1).

### Choose deep relationships over shallow illusions.

I have a small group of close friends whom I trust with seeing my flaws, to pray over my sin, and to share the ups and downs of an authentic life. Barry and a handful of women know me fully and still love me wholeheartedly. Their love never fails to amaze me! When even one person in my space knows me beyond any image I've chosen to construct, depth of relationship is sure to follow. It's both scary and soul-satisfying!

I was recently challenged to confront the issues of a troubled relationship. Day after day I wanted to walk away, and one day I even composed an e-mail that would have effectively ended the relationship.

Thankfully, I didn't click the send button that day. I saved the e-mail in my drafts folder and simmered. Finally, I sought the counsel of godly, wise friends. They gently but faithfully pointed out that not only was I defaulting to my "competent" label, I was giving in to my Good Girl tendency to flee rather than having a difficult, problem-solving conversation. My insightful friends encouraged me to give the relationship a fighting chance, instead of retreating to retain my shallow label.

I opted for the hard conversation instead of the e-mail and was grateful to have ultimately chosen a deeper relationship over a pleasant façade. It felt great to break up with the idea of the perfect situation rather than ending a friendship that's grown through the hard time. The positive result of that hard conversation gives me faith that it works to pursue depth and authenticity in relationships. I won't be so afraid to come out from behind my mask in the future.

## IN GOD'S HANDS

It's good to know that we perfectionists can put our can-do hearts at rest and trust our image entirely in God's hands. When we confidently step into the image God delighted in when He dreamed us up, being well thought of by those around us holds little allure. And who are we to construct a flawed replica of the woman God created anyway? In God's hands, our image is honed and polished to a glow. In His hands we become fully and gloriously human. Our gifts become blessings. Our personalities grow delightful. Even our flaws and failures are transformed into stories to glorify the One who redeems them.

But if we insist on constructing our own image of perfection, people will respond to us in one of two ways: they will be either attracted or repelled. Neither option results in a happy ending. The ones who are attracted are only allowed to get so close, because if they get too close, our image of perfection will be shattered by the inevitable flaws revealed by everyday life. The ones who are repelled either catch a whiff of fake or feel they can never live up to the image we portray. Those are terrible options. Instead, let's lean into the God of Rachel, Leah, and Tamar, the God who redeems women's stories and images. He's the God who created us in His own image and beckons us to give up our own. He gives us a perfected image rooted in our identity as a child of the perfect God.

For this girl, breaking up with the desire to create myself in my own image is one of the biggest struggles I have. I wish I could tell you that I'm completely over it, but just this week I got an e-mail that sent me into a tailspin. In it, the sender questioned a decision I made to speak for an online conference in which I was one of just a handful of Christians. The majority of speakers represented worldviews diametrically opposed to what I believe to be true. Although my own message was true to the message of God as the source of everything good, I was misunderstood, critiqued, and judged. As soon as I got the e-mail, my day was derailed. My stomach dropped, and I worried obsessively about how others would perceive my choice and how it would affect my image as a Christian woman/speaker/writer.

I'm growing, though. After several hours of agonizing, I finally dropped to my face in front of the One who knows my heart. I cried out to Him to forgive me if I had made a poor decision and asked for His protection from misunderstanding. As I lingered in God's presence, He reassured me that He sees my genuine motives and my desire to be true to my image-bearer identity. My heart quieted, and I realized that three-dimensional, Jesus-loving girls don't have to be afraid of a sullied image. My identity as a whole woman is based on God's strength shown in me. Yours is too.

## Transformation Points

1. What group of people have you molded your image to fit, either now or in the past?

2. How was that image different from your truest self?

3. What do you think would change if you were fully bearing God's image instead of shaping your own?

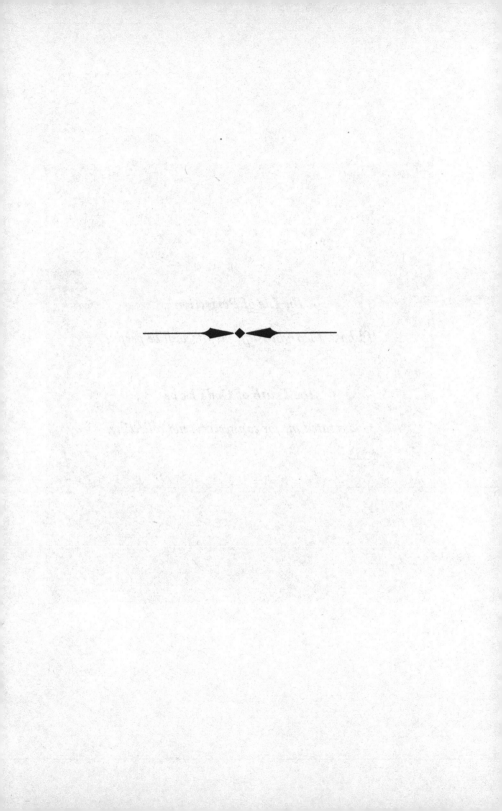

**The Lie of Perfection**

*If I have the right stuff, my life will be perfect.*

**The Truth of God's Love**

*God created me for connecting, not collecting.*

## Chapter Five

# HEARTBREAK HOTEL

*Connecting with People Rather Than Collecting Stuff*

Signs for your house are the rage, and I'm obsessed with them. Peppered around the rooms of our home are plaques, pictures, and pillows with sayings I love, reminding me of what I value and how I need to grow. One says "Plant Joy." Another one that makes me giggle every time I look at it reads, "What if the hokey pokey *is* what it's all about?" The love chapter of the Bible, 1 Corinthians 13, printed in the shape of a heart by a beloved friend, hangs by my back door. Most of my signs make me smile, but the one that pierces my heart each time I read it reminds me of an ongoing struggle. An aged board sitting on my breakfast bar boldly states, "For a happy life, want what you have."

Like most people, I have to work to push down the desire screaming for more, more, more in a consumer culture. Americans are famous for using our stuff to build a persona and shape our image, but we perfectionists might be the worst. Remembering that the *love* of money is the root of all kinds of evil (1 Timothy 6:10)—not the money itself—maybe we could say the perfectionist's love of stuff to create a façade is the root of her problem, rather than the stuff itself. We perfectionists use our material goods either to feel perfect or to look acceptable to others.

T-shirts printed with "The one who dies with the most toys wins" and sayings like "Keeping up with the Joneses" make us laugh, but they're no joke. We use our cars, our houses, and our clothes to tell people who we are, and each generation seems to increasingly depend on material things to define themselves. "Compared with Americans in 1957, today we own twice as many cars per person, eat out twice as often and enjoy endless other commodities that weren't around then—big-screen TVs, microwave ovens, SUVs and handheld wireless devices, to name a few,"[1] reports Tori DeAngelis of the American Psychological Association.

## FLUFFING AND REFEATHERING

Some trends toward materialism puzzle me. I shake my head at the cost of designer clothes and handbags, while I sort through the racks of thrift stores with glee. I stick generic brands of groceries into my cart without blinking an eye. The redneck, homemade TV antenna my guys made from a template on the Internet serves as artwork in our living room while I am content to watch only network TV and merrily pay no cable bill each month. Although I'm a cheapskate in some areas, I wouldn't dare judge you if those are places you spend your money. Making my home look nice is where I continue to wrestle with materialism. My home is the nest I love to fluff and refeather regularly. It makes me both smile and cringe to recall buying the sign on my breakfast bar that helps me remember not to buy so much. I obviously haven't arrived.

For six years my lust for all things home and garden was amped up by a job I held with the local welcome service. As I explained to my friends, it was a job where I was "paid to be perky" while I did a warm-fuzzy brand of advertising in people's new homes. I'd scan my list of all the new residents of my town, knock on their door with my cute basket of goodies hanging on my arm, and then when I was invited inside, I'd give

> *Too often my wanter exposes my love for what can't love me back.*

them the skinny on our Southern town and its wonderful businesses. While we chatted, I cased the joint. Unfortunately, my inner dialogue wasn't nearly as people-focused as the conversation I was having with the homeowner. *Wow, look at those beautiful granite countertops. That crown molding is gorgeous and should have its own zip code! Those hand-scraped hardwoods would look great in my house . . . love them!*

Every day my desire for more, bigger, and better was stoked to a roaring fire. I'd return home with a critical eye and an unsatisfied heart. It didn't take long for me to recognize my old buddies Covetousness and Discontent sidling up to me for one more round of "This Too Could Be Yours!" By now it's a well-worn path toward a familiar trap, so I've learned from hard experience what to do. I needed to ask myself why I craved those things and to readjust my "wanter." The focus of our wants reveals what we truly love and value; too often my wanter exposes my love for what can't love me back.

## DERAILED

Years ago, my family moved into a fixer-upper just outside a historic district in our town, and I loved every puke-green inch of it. The floors were green. The tile was green. The walls were green, and even the ceilings we had believed were white had a tint of green that revealed itself as we painted the walls a buttercream yellow. I launched into high gear to update our new-to-us home. Dragging my toddler and newborn in my wake, I led an attack on every home store, paint supplier, and décor shop in the area. My mind, heart, and time filled with paint chips, wallpaper books, flooring samples, and fabric swatches. I loved it all and reveled in every moment. Doing it on a shoestring budget didn't feel daunting. It felt like a challenge, and I was determined to design a champagne home on a watered-down-beer budget. My home had become my identity—the way I wanted to represent myself to the world—so it needed to look good.

One morning I paused in the midst of paint fumes, half-stripped wallpaper, and the enormous mess that consumed the whole house every time we worked on a room. In the silence, I felt God drawing me to spend time with Him, so I dug my Bible out from under a mound of decorating magazines and sat waiting for His voice. The whisper came almost immediately. "You have an idol," my Father gently said. *An idol?*

My imagination flooded with carved images painted with bright colors and pagans worshipping in a circle, but it only took a quick glance around the room to see the trappings of my distracting god. I surveyed the squares of five shades of beige painted on the wall, the strips of fabric samples on the chair, and the pile of magazines from under which I had just extricated my Bible. My quest for the perfect home was drowning my first love for God by drips. My focus had shifted, and I needed God's rebuke to begin an about-face. It wasn't too strong to say that decorating had become my idol. It had shoved

God out of preeminence, and I only had to look at the number of days I had ignored my Bible to know the truth.

In that moment, I acutely felt my need for change but also the powerlessness to create the momentum change would take. My faithful God continued to give instructions. Cancel cable with the allure of HGTV. Unsubscribe to *Better Homes and Gardens* and *Southern Living* with their pictures of luscious rooms. Limit the shopping and restrain the doing. The ideas coming at me were clearly not my own, because they were darts into the heart of my household dreams. However, I knew God was asking me to sacrifice with a purpose. He wanted me to turn away from my idol completely so I could live my greatest purpose—living in seamless connection to Him.

For Jesus-loving girls, it seems so silly to get to the place of elevating Prada, Porsche, iPod, or Pottery Barn onto the thrones of our hearts. Good Girls amass things to please and fit in. Never Good Enough Girls collect to hide behind a barricade of purchased acceptability. We know better. We want better. But in the pursuit of the perfect life, we often get derailed by the American dream. Our perfection-seeking hearts just can't seem to resist one more purchase. That's when we must turn our focus away from our mound of materialism and back to the Perfect One.

## OTHER LOVES AND OTHERS' STUFF

Recently, the multiage women's small group I co-teach went through the Ten Commandments. I suddenly grasped the exquisite simplicity of these streamlined laws for the very first time. Our God gave us only ten heart-shaping commands for loving well, and they completely cover the issues of the human race. The first two commandments address our stuff-lust in relation to Him.

In Exodus 20:3–6, God demands:

*You shall have no other gods before me. You shall not make for yourself an image in the form of anything in heaven above or on the earth beneath or in the waters below. You shall not bow down to them or worship them; for I, the LORD your God, am a jealous God, punishing the children for the sin of the parents to the third and fourth generation of those who hate me, but showing love to a thousand generations of those who love me and keep my commandments.*

Where does God get the authority to draw such dividing lines in our motives? He clearly establishes His right in verse two when He says, "I am the LORD your God, who brought you out of Egypt, out of the land of slavery." My heart stands up and cries "Yes!" in response. Being freed from this particular Egypt—the pursuit of Perfect—is freedom from a cruel slave driver. The God Who makes us and frees us, the God Who loves us boundlessly and knows how we function best, the God Who is full of grace for those who love Him—this God has the right to establish Himself as first and His ways as highest.

In these verses, God gives us two choices that reveal His best for us. We can love Him, or we can hate Him. Hate Him? That seems extreme, but Jesus also says this plainly in the case of money, the agent that buys us all the stuff creating our false façade. "No one can serve two masters. Either you will hate the one and love the other, or you will be devoted to the one and despise the other. You cannot serve both God and money" (Matthew 6:24). We have a clear decision to make. Choosing our material trappings as first in our life over God is not an innocuous choice. The walls of image and safety that we build with material goods block our relationship with Him.

In her book 7, Jen Hatmaker says it this way: "Do not be fooled by the luxuries of this world; they cripple our faith. As Jesus explained, the right things have to die so the right things can live—we die to selfishness, greed, power, accumulation, prestige, and self-preservation, giving life to community, generosity, compassion, mercy, brotherhood, kindness, and love."[2] Then Jen leads right into the commandment where God addresses all we have and our craving for more: "You shall not covet your neighbor's house. You shall not covet your neighbor's wife, or his male or female servant, his ox or donkey, or anything that belongs to your neighbor" (Exodus 20:17).

My. Oh. My. Now, why does God have to start with houses? It's almost like He knows the future and sees HGTV being beamed into my living room. It's as if He perceives my house-coveting heart and the welcome-service job coming down the pike. It really does make me want to stick my lip out in a big ol' pout, but He pegs my heart without flinching.

## CHOOSING WHAT CONNECTS

Here's the bottom line. We're created for connecting, not collecting. God, our relationship-initiating Father, knows that collecting homes, tchotchkes, cars, clothes, tech gadgets, and all the rest of it keeps our hearts engaged in the temporal. We girls who are trying to form a perfect life so often use our possessions to define us, but those things are just building blocks for a perfect, empty box. Relationships, as messy as they are, fill the rooms of our lives with love, laughter, joy, and unbreakable bonds in a way our inanimate gods never could.

It's an extreme example, but I think about the TV show *Hoarders*. You've probably watched in horror—just as I have—as cameras capture homes filled floor to ceiling with newspapers, collections of every sort, clothes, boxes with the price tags still on them, trash, and every other material thing imaginable, with only a narrow path leading from room to room. As the hoarder's massive collection grows, spilling over into living areas and filling up every nook and cranny, family members move out and relationships are strained, sometimes to the point of complete estrangement. Meanwhile, in miserable loneliness, the hoarder is trapped both physically and emotionally by the very things he or she craves. The show gives us a visual illustration of a problem that can invade our hearts in a less visible but no less damaging way. When we prioritize material things, we minimize deeper relationships. However, God gives us three powerful antidotes to the effects of materialism: *simplicity*, *generosity*, and *gratitude*.

*We're created for connecting, not collecting.*

## Simplicity

Although my inner decorator loves layers of girly abundance, I'm beginning to see simplicity as a blessing. Embracing simplicity allows us to live more life with less excess. As Chuck Palahniuk insightfully says, "The more things you own, the more they own you." Visions of family and friends spending idyllic days on the water may seem like a fantastic idea until boat insurance, slip fees, and repairs start to sink your budget. The idea of entering your high school reunion in those Jimmy Choos may be captivating—until the credit card bill arrives. Personally, I dream of riding with the top down in my zippy convertible (I *will* have one before I die, even if I only have one gray hair blowing in the breeze), but right now I need to pay tuition bills instead. It's not wrong to have some dreams of special things, but that ragtop will have to wait until it's not a weight.

When we moved out of our dream fixer-upper ten years ago into a much more expensive housing market, we downsized our square footage dramatically. Our move required a major cleaning-out and giving-away stage as we packed boxes. Unpacking in the new house revealed a need to do a second wave of purging to fit into the diminished space, and before Christmas that year I did a third round of eliminating. Several months later, I came to a startling conclusion. I couldn't remember one item I had given away. Not one. It was an enormous "aha moment." The leaner life is a more ideal life. There was less to pay for, less to maintain, and best of all, less to dust!

## Generosity

Generosity is the natural outflow of a simpler life. The more open-handed we are with our stuff, the more delighted we are to find someone who will be blessed in receiving it. Suddenly, looking for ways to invest our excess seems much more ideal than hoarding it. In 2012, the US Census reported that the median annual income is $50,502.[3] That means that the average American makes just over 138 dollars a day. Shockingly, the World Bank reported in 2008 that 80 percent of the world lives on less than 10 dollars a day.[4] Fifteen percent live on less than one dollar a day.[5] These statistics show a world of overwhelming need, and we have a lot to share. I think we need to ask ourselves, how much of our riches do we acquire in order to create an externally perfect life? The truth is that our lives would be more truly perfect if we held on to less and reveled more in the gift of giving.

Years ago the president of the Proverbs 31 Ministries team challenged us to give up one family night out in a restaurant to sponsor a child through Compassion International. Our family tradition has changed as my boys have grown, but in those early days of our sponsorship, we created a fun night each month. We'd roll our beans and rice in tortillas; bow our heads to pray for our sponsored child, Manuel; and write letters to him. Our family made sweet memories together while we focused on others rather than ourselves. We learned an important truth as we sacrificed a little to gain a huge blessing. Generosity breeds joy—both for the giver and the receiver.

## Gratitude

There's nothing like generosity to help make us grateful. And gratitude is the cure for the nasty sin of covetousness. When I begin to see everything I have as provision from the Master Gift Giver instead of listing all the items missing from my picture of perfect, my wanter really does begin to change. Instead of coveting—wanting what I don't have—gratitude shifts my focus to what I do have. Suddenly, I'm operating from a sense of abundance with a desire to give—a trait that leads to beautiful relationships—instead of a feeling of lack, which makes me want to take.

## EXCEPTIONAL WISDOM IN AN UNEXPECTED PLACE

God taught me one of the greatest lessons of simplicity, generosity, and gratitude while I was visiting a humble blue cinder-block house in the mountains of Ecuador. Early on a Sunday morning, our Proverbs 31 team loaded into buses that drove us out of the large capital city of Quito, into the gorgeous countryside, and eventually further up the mountains. I watched

*There's nothing like generosity to help make us grateful.*

with my nose pressed against the window while green fields, dark volcanoes, shimmering lakes, and acres of hothouses filled with roses rolled by. As the bus gained altitude, our group exclaimed at the majesty of the mountains and the small, neatly rowed fields terraced on the slopes.

Suddenly, the bus rounded a corner on the twisting mountain road, and the stucco church with the red-tiled roof where we were to attend a service came into view. Our group clambered down the steps and walked toward the church flanked on either side by two rows of stunning, dark-haired, dark-eyed children clad in heavily embroidered clothing. With nervous grins, the children handed us roses as we walked by. But it didn't take long for their shyness to disappear, and they climbed into our laps and held our hands throughout the service.

When the sermon ended, our Compassion International hosts gathered us around to unveil our afternoon agenda. Our team was to split into pairs with an in-country host to do home visits with the children. They explained that the beautiful faces of these children might cause us to overlook the harsh reality of their lives. So, carrying groceries for the families, we set out to visit their homes and see their true living conditions.

My friend Luann and I climbed into the back of a small red pickup truck for our journey to Dolores's house. Down a small track we rode. When the narrow road ended, we continued on foot up a path, past a field of maize with a rooting pig tied to a rope, until we reached the house. Dolores greeted us and invited us in to meet her family. Her husband, a builder working in Quito, wasn't there that day, but evidently they had a loving relationship when he was home. He and Dolores had filled their tiny space with seven children!

Being a lover of houses, I did a mental appraisal during the short tour. The home was tidy, but the floors were bare dirt, and plastic sheeting served as a ceiling. There was running water and electricity but no appliances for work in the kitchen. The only sign of food was a small stack of maize in the corner. In the bedroom, we saw two beds for the whole family, and though the mountain nights and winters must be cold, I didn't see a furnace or any indications that the house was heated. Even so, it was obvious that Dolores was proud of her well-built home and of the hours her faithful husband had spent building it for their family. She glowed as she described the care and craftsmanship he invested for them.

As the visit was winding up, my precious prayer-warrior friend Luann asked Dolores the pivotal question: "Dolores," Luann began, "we are never going to forget you. When we go home, we want to be able to ask our friends to pray for you. How can we pray for you and your family? What is your greatest need?"

The interpreter repeated the question in Spanish. While we waited for Dolores's reply to be repeated in English, I had a little talk with God based on my own assessments of her lack. Looking around her tiny three-room house, I created a mental list of things she needed. "Lord, Dolores needs more beds so she doesn't wake up with elbows and knees digging into her head all night long. She needs a refrigerator so food will keep between visits to the faraway market. She needs some carpet on her dirt floor to keep the family's feet warm during the cold nights in the mountains. She needs a four-wheel-drive to make it down the dirt track that leads to her house. She needs a solid roof and ceiling to keep the rain out . . ." My list for Dolores went on and on until the interpreter finally began to speak to Luann and me.

My mouth hung open as I listened to Dolores's response: "My greatest need is to be able to teach my children about Jesus so they will follow the Lord all the days of their lives." Tears sprang to my eyes as my heart absorbed the lesson this Ecuadorian woman in humble circumstances taught me. All of my basic needs are met, and even many of my wants are met with abundance. In spite of all my blessings, my priorities are all mixed up. Dolores found great joy living in the simplicity of her home with her basic needs met. Her gratitude for her husband's provision was beautiful, and she displayed great generosity in asking for her children instead of herself when asked her greatest need. Dolores held the gifts of simplicity, generosity, and gratitude. Because her wanter was set in the right direction, this mother knew the most important thing her family needed. She knew they all needed Jesus. He came first on her list for herself and for her children.

King David expressed his desire for knowing the Lord this way:

> *How lovely is your dwelling place,*
> *LORD Almighty!*
> *My soul yearns, even faints*
>     *for the courts of the LORD;*
> *my heart and my flesh cry out*
>     *for the living God. . . .*
> *Better is one day in your courts*
>     *than a thousand elsewhere;*
> *I would rather be a doorkeeper in the house of my God*
>     *than dwell in the tents of the wicked.*

> (Psalm 84:1–2, 10)

In essence, our Ecuadorian friend had said the same thing. Dolores wanted to spend her life in the Lord's dwelling place more than she wanted a spacious, beautiful home. She wanted to be in His courts more than she wanted to have a powerful position. She wanted to know the fullness of Jesus more than she wanted to leave her spare situation.

I'm sorry to say that I wondered what my response would be to the questions "What is your greatest need? How can I pray for you?" I do love the Lord, but sometimes He falls to less than first place on my list of perceived needs. A woman with limited education but tremendous wisdom had reminded me of a great truth. She gave my wanter a major adjustment, and I walked away with something far greater than the bag of groceries that I had brought in. My picture of perfection shifted away from a material façade and toward a life full of the riches of a deeper relationship with Jesus and others.

## Transformation Points

1. Read 1 Kings 3:1–14. Why did God appear to Solomon in a dream and offer Solomon whatever he wanted?

2. Read verse 9 from The Message alongside your usual translation: "Here's what I want: Give me a God-listening heart so I can lead your people well, discerning the difference between good and evil. For who on their own is capable of leading your glorious people?" (1 Kings 3:9, The Message). What can we learn from what Solomon wanted more than anything?

———◆———

### The Lie of Perfection

*I don't need anyone else—*
*I'm totally self-sufficient.*

### The Truth of God's Love

*God created me for community—*
*to both give and receive.*

*Chapter Six*

# WE ARE NEVER GETTING BACK TOGETHER

*Breaking Up with Our Independent Self*

All of a sudden, a friend in my weekly women's class at church came into our group missing her usual smile and encouraging words. Her walk had lost its spring, and her hard-gained wisdom—which she usually shared freely—had gone into hiding. After a few weeks of this, she and I finally had a conversation after class one day. She poured out the heartache she was living in as her extended family battled around her. My heart joined with hers in sympathy, and I asked permission to call her once a week to check in and pray. Tears flowing and head nodding, she admitted she could use the regular contact and boost.

Our weekly calls during that time focused on her family crisis, and we met the pain together, our tears coupling with prayers. Several months later, after the worst of the problems had been resolved and our calls had tapered off, my phone rang one afternoon. I was cheered to hear my friend's voice on the other end. "I heard your prayer request in class this week," she said. "I know your son is struggling, and I understand how painful it is to have your children hurt. How's it going? Can I pray for both of you?"

This time I was the one who cried grateful tears as she reached out to pray. The ache in my heart lightened as I reveled in the words of faith directed heavenward and the deep connection we had forged. My friend had proven herself true—she was able to both give and receive in season. I have to be honest. I felt a bit uncomfortable when I gave up my position of "ministering to" and stepped into the role of "*being* ministered to." But as I settled into my new role of receiving, I discovered that it really was nice to soak up the comfort she shared.

> *For perfectionists, receiving is uncomfortable and a threat to our image, even if we're in desperate need.*

Why is it so hard for us perfectionists to receive? It seems so much easier to give. Unfortunately, sometimes our pursuit of perfection and our competitive nature keep us from the kind of sharing that involves both give and take. We want to be the best employee, the best Sunday school teacher, the best wife, or the best PTA member. We want to prove we know how to do it best, and so we do everything—all by ourselves. Receiving is uncomfortable and a threat to our perfect image, even if we're in desperate need.

For women who wrestle in the web of perfectionism, giving comes naturally. That's what nice people do, right? They give and give and give. When I was discussing the theme of this book with a friend, she exclaimed, "Oh my goodness! What woman doesn't struggle with perfectionism?! We're expected to take care of everything and everyone without a thought to ourselves." I've felt the exact same pressure my friend expressed.

Out of the hope that people will love us more and the fear that we won't give enough to be accepted, we work our fingers to the bone. But in the midst of those culturally imposed, unrealistic expectations, my inner rebel rises up. People might want us to do it all, but is it really what God requires? He hasn't made us to go it alone, and trying to do life with no help can have disastrous outcomes.

## A MISSION MESS

A former pastor of mine says people fall into one of two categories, "be-ers" and "do-ers." Be-ers are those who are charged up by quiet time with God and others. They are comfortable in their own skin, and they refuel with prayer and reflection. Do-ers are energized by action and completing their list. Self-sufficiency is their hallmark, and they're always on the go. It doesn't take too much to figure out where most perfectionists land. I'm definitely a do-er, and I'll bet you're in the same tribe.

In the summer of my twentieth year, my do-er wiring was almost my undoing. I went on a summer mission trip that year as the assistant leader of a group of teenagers. Looking back, I'm horrified. The leader of the trip, Pam, was a godly twenty-one-year-old, and off we went with seven teenagers across the ocean to Scotland for the summer. There is absolutely no way I would send my own teens off with leaders just a few years older than them, but back in the day I didn't think twice about my ability to lead. Just once, when I glimpsed "In

Case of Death on the Field" in the leader's handbook, I had a flicker of uncertainty. But I shoved doubt aside, picked up my can-do attitude, checked my massive list, and felt sure I had it all together.

During the course of the summer, Pam and I fell into our natural roles, and we were given nicknames to fit. She was Praying Pam, and I was Action Amy. While Pam was more deliberate and cautious and determined to pray before any decision was made, I was confident of my own ability to get 'er done. I worked and fixed and reprimanded with ease, until the day I realized that my nickname wasn't a compliment.

One day on the way to our work site, Pam confronted me with the feelings of the group. "They think you're bossy," she said, "and they don't like it. You take over every situation. You don't listen, and you don't let them give of their gifts." Sobbing, I left the group to spend the day in the park alone to reflect and pray. Even now, I remember that day as one of the worst and most painful of my life.

Don't feel sorry for me, though. Pam's critique was harsh, but it was fair. Feeling the self-imposed pressure to be self-sufficient and strong, I had stripped the others in the group of their right to give of themselves. I wanted things to be perfect, and in my mind-set that meant doing all the work and allowing my overdeveloped sense of responsibility to run wild. Hearing our kids didn't like me was heartbreaking. I had damaged relationships when my intent was to make sure *everything* was well for *everyone*.

> *Feeling the self-imposed pressure to be self-sufficient and strong, I had stripped the others in the group of their right to give of themselves.*

In reality, Pam and I were probably pretty well paired. There's a need for both prayer and action, right? We each needed to implement a little of what the other had to attain equilibrium, and our personalities balanced the leadership team as a whole. However, from that difficult day forward, I tried to live out what I had learned—even though the learning process had been painful. I reined in my do-er tendencies and tried to embrace more be-er traits. I did less and encouraged the kids to step up so their gifts shone. I instructed little and listened much. I discussed rather than reprimanding. Much to my surprise, in the process of growing personally, I started receiving as much as I gave. The kids reached out to me with forgiveness, and our relationships grew. The group healed and began to develop a true sense of community. I think the kids even liked me a little by the end! The lesson I learned that summer was excruciating but essential. Perfection cripples community. Healthy interdependence builds it.

## A TIME FOR REAPING

"God's ways are always best" was a phrase repeated over and over by my little boys' children's pastor, and it's amazing how it continues to stick in my mind too. When we build strong community through the power of sharing, we are simply tapping into an ancient God-established truth. "Remember this: Whoever sows sparingly will also reap sparingly, and whoever sows generously will also reap generously" (2 Corinthians 9:6).

According to Ecclesiastes, there's a season for everything, including reaping and sowing. While sowing is a time of working, giving, and putting in sweat equity, reaping is a time for receiving back in abundance. There is truly a time and a need in our souls for giving, but there's also an often-neglected but necessary time for receiving. Sharing is a concept that implies both giving and receiving. Giving is the mark of charity, and charity is a virtue; however, always giving while never receiving is a lonely, one-sided deal. In contrast, giving and receiving in season creates community.

We weren't created to do life independently, and we desperately need community. Consider God's ancient truth expressed in Ecclesiastes 4:9–12:

> *Two are better than one,*
> > *because they have a good return for their labor:*
> *If either of them falls down,*
> > *one can help the other up.*
> *But pity anyone who falls*
> > *and has no one to help them up!*
> *Also, if two lie down together, they will keep warm.*
> > *But how can one keep warm alone?*
> *Though one may be overpowered,*
> > *two can defend themselves.*
> *A cord of three strands is not quickly broken.*

Two has always been better than one, and helping has always been part of a union.

As reforming perfectionists, it's our default to prove ourselves by doing it all on our own, but in doing that, we rob ourselves. Look back at some of the powerful words and phrases in the Ecclesiastes passage: *good return, help, keep warm, defend, not quickly broken.* We deny ourselves the security of being part of a group if we constantly assert our independence, and we steal the joy of giving from others.

For a perfectionist, it takes intentionality to move away from our burning need to do it all. When my friend offered to pray for my son and me, I had to allow myself to feel my need—rather than numbing my pain by working to meet everyone else's need. And then I had to accept the fact that I hurt.

So many times I push back against a felt need because I'm trying to prove my Superwoman status. Until we perfectionists accept the fact that we're weak like everyone else, we won't be able to go to the final step of receiving. We've got to relax a little, let our friends and family have their turn in the giving-receiving cycle, and bask in the feeling of being cherished.

## RECEIVING THE BLESSING OF COMMUNITY

God Himself is a triune spirit living in perfect, loving community. It's an unfathomable mystery, but the Father, the Son, and the Holy Spirit reveal the very essence of God in a unified group. Living in the giving and receiving tides of community displays the image of our God to the world.

In the thirteenth chapter of the book of Hebrews, God gives us a beautiful view of community in His church and the outpouring of sharing.

*Keep on loving each other as brothers and sisters. Do not forget to show hospitality to strangers, for by so doing some people have shown hospitality to angels without knowing it. Continue to remember those in prison as if you were together with them in prison, and those who are mistreated as if you yourselves were suffering. Marriage should be honored by all . . . So we say with confidence, "The LORD is my helper; I will not be afraid. What can mere mortals do to me?" Remember your leaders, who spoke the word of God to you. Consider the outcome of their way of life and imitate their faith.*

(Hebrews 13:1–4a, 6–7)

In the richness of these verses, we get a glimpse into the multiple facets of community—those bound together as brothers and sisters in faith—strangers, prisoners, mistreated people, married couples, leaders, and God Himself presiding over all. This group is encouraged to be interwoven by love, hospitality, remembrance, and honor. I love this picture of each person living in the fullness of their roles, sometimes receiving help, as in the case of the mistreated, prisoners, and strangers, and sometimes giving it.

I'm looking out the window as I read these verses and write, thinking about my neighbors and friends. I love how we each function in our sphere of influence, and how God calls us to live out the truths of community even today. You can probably match up many of the roles from the verses above with the people in your little corner of the world.

## AN UNFAILING SOURCE

As in the time the book of Hebrews was written, the Lord Himself is in the middle of our community and is reliable as a faithful helper. The word *helper* used in verse six is fascinating because it's the same word used to describe Eve in Genesis 2:18. The Hebrew word *ezer*, translated as "helper," not only was used to refer to a woman in relation to her husband, but it refers to God's role in relation to us! In this picture, God is serving us, and we are called to be the recipients of His help.

I've always thought of "helper" as a subordinate role, but here in Hebrews it's a mighty word that inspires the author to say, "I will not be afraid. What can mere mortals do to me?" As God's child, I always saw myself as *His* helper or servant. But God calls us to receive help from Him—as our *ezer*—and it's a strong and saving help.

> *In this picture, God is serving us, and we are called to be the recipients of His help.*

From the very first breath of life that He breathed into us, we've been dependent on Him, so why do we struggle so hard for self-sufficiency? Scripture tells us that . . .

- He's the giver of every good and perfect gift (James 1:17).
- He's a father who loves to give when His children ask (Matthew 7:11).
- He gives us the shield of victory, and His hand sustains us (Psalm 18:35).
- He gives us the desires of our hearts (Psalm 37:4).
- He lavishes us with grace (Ephesians 1:7–8).
- He pours out everlasting love (Jeremiah 31:3).

This list is just a drop in the ocean of God's gifts that help us through this life. If you and I are willing to open our hearts to *freely receive* God's help rather than *working to earn* His help, then He will joyfully equip us with what we need.

## A COMMUNITY WOVEN IN SUFFERING

Linda and I were part of the same church community, but I first met her in difficult circumstances. As a young mom myself, I held the usually happy job of visiting the new moms in our congregation to offer them a gift, some prayer, and a little mom-to-mom encouragement. This time was different, though. "Amy," the church secretary said when she called to alert me of a needed mom visit, "Linda is receiving cancer treatments along with taking care of her newborn." I was heavy-hearted as I drove to visit this young woman who had been diagnosed with a rare and aggressive breast cancer during her first trimester. When the baby was safe in the third trimester, Linda had begun chemo, so she was experiencing postpartum recovery as well as the fatigue of treatments.

Once I was in the room with Linda, however, my gloom evaporated. Even in her weakened state, Linda was full of life and joy. We ooohed and ahhhhed over our baby boys, who were almost the same age, and compared notes on their older brothers. It was the beginning of a treasured friendship. I'd love to say I was an encouragement to Linda and her family, but the truth is that she was the one who taught me. She showed me how to live through suffering completely dependent on God and those around you. She proclaimed God's glory and goodness every day of her life. Linda was vibrant, loving, full of faith, and willing to receive the help of others.

For three blessed years, I walked with Linda through her battle with cancer—treatments, a short remission, a desperate bone-marrow transplant—until Linda died. I was devastated. It was a time of wrestling with God and asking Him the big questions. How could You let this happen, God? Where were You when the first cancer cell invaded a woman whose womb was full? How will this little family of a man and his two boys survive without their precious mama?

One day, less than a month after Linda's funeral, there was a knock on my door. I was shocked to see Don, Linda's husband, standing on my porch with a bag in his hand. "I know how much you're struggling with Linda's death, Amy," he said, "so I brought you a book that's helped me a lot." I was stunned. Here was a man in the midst of the greatest tragedy of his life reaching out to me. I knew the roles should have been reversed, but I thankfully took the book he offered.

Poring over page after page of the healing words, there was one fact that stood out from all the others. The author explained that when people are in crisis or suffering, they most often "circle the wagons," drawing close to those who are known and loved while keeping all others outside. Slowly, I began to realize what a great gift I had been given. Instead of closing inward during Linda's sickness, Don and Linda had done the exact opposite. It seemed as if everyone in our whole town had been drawn into their sweet family circle. Churches, Bible studies, and prayer groups all over town had prayed for Linda. One group at church paid for housecleaning while another set of friends organized meals. Linda's mother made several cross-country, long-term visits when the family needed her, and she became one of us. Everywhere Linda's family went, they loved people lavishly and allowed others to love them by helping.

Linda couldn't do it all, and she didn't even try. Instead of trying to be self-sufficient and image conscious, Linda created the most beautiful, extensive community I've ever seen in the midst of the worst suffering of her life. Every year at Christmas I wear the angel pin she gave to a group of her friends toward the end of her life, and I remember. I don't remember her last days of tremendous pain. I don't remember all the side effects of chemo. I don't remember her family's tear-stained faces. All those realities aren't forgotten, but they're wrapped around an exquisite package. It's Linda's life as a whole, lived in the midst of a vibrant, loving community, that I remember with both stabs of pain and great joy.

I'm never getting back together with my do-er mentality. "I'll do it myself" has been replaced with "Let's do it together." God helping. Others supporting. Ebb and flow. Giving and receiving. That's the pattern of community, and it's the habit I want to cultivate for life. Join me here! I'm finding it's a delightful place to live, so the allure of self-sufficiency diminishes daily.

Relationships with friends and family flourish with mutual generosity, and my relationship with God becomes all it can be when I let go of trying to pull myself up by my bootstraps. Instead of working to receive, a mind-set God never meant to be, the sower-reaper life is filled with praise and gratitude. In the end, those are the priceless gifts I give to God, and even they are the result of His outpouring to me. So I stand here with a big smile on my face and my hands open wide. They're hands that are ready to help if you're in need or ready to receive what you've got to give. Let's relinquish our need to do it all and exchange it for the joy and abundance that community brings.

> *I'm never getting back together with my do-er mentality.*

## Transformation Points

1. How would you rate yourself at receiving help from others?

2. What keeps you from being a good receiver? How does your answer connect with your Good Girl List or Never Good Enough List?

3. Who do you consider to be part of your community if you accept this definition: "Giving and receiving in season creates community"?

4. How might you add to the list of those in your community?

———◆—◆———

*Part Three*

# BREAKING UP WITH
# SELFISH ACTIONS

*Getting Free from What Consumes Our Days*

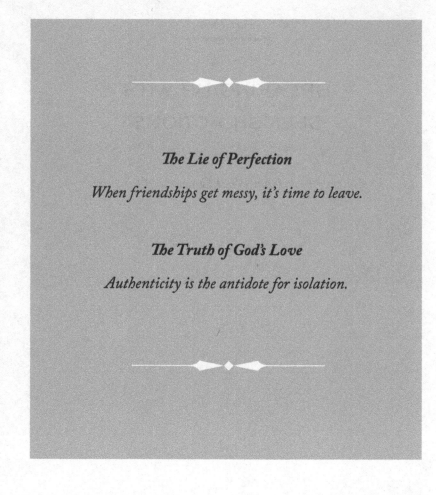

**The Lie of Perfection**

*When friendships get messy, it's time to leave.*

**The Truth of God's Love**

*Authenticity is the antidote for isolation.*

*Chapter Seven*

## ALL BY MYSELF

*Exchanging Perfect for Friendship*

As much as I love community, there's something else that fuels me even more, and I'll bet you can relate. I adore one-on-one time with my girlfriends. It's how I love to fill my days. I truly wish you and I could sit down over coffee and get to know each other. We'd do the girly stuff, like talking about our favorite kind of chocolate, and then we'd move on to discussing the best days of our lives and the dreams in our hearts. We would bond as we shared the hardest days, too, and each one of us could encourage the other by telling how God showed up during the dark times. Over time and with open hearts, we'd build a friendship. I know we would.

But inevitably, just because we're human, things would begin to get messy as we moved down the road of our friendship. I'd say something that hurt your feelings. You'd forget to show up for our latest scheduled lunch. Another friend would enter our circle, and some competition or jealousy would fire up. I'd do something that earned your disapproval, and then you'd do the same. Slowly but surely, just like the fabled Chinese water torture, our friendship would be damaged by drips. Hurt . . . drip. Jealousy . . . drip. Competition . . . drip. Drip. Drip. Drip.

Because I like things perfect and so do you, messy just isn't where we like to live, so the erosion of our friendship would get too uncomfortable. It doesn't fit on my Good Girl List, and you might add it to your Never Good Enough List. I won't have a big blowup with you. I'm just too Southern-belle to do loud conflict. We won't end things with a knock-down, drag-out fight, but one day you'll turn around and wonder when I disappeared. "Where'd she go?" you'll ask yourself. And I'll have snuck out the "back door" into the safety of isolation.

How do I know this? Because this has been a repeated pattern in my life. I wouldn't fight with you, but when less-than-perfect enters and things get messy, I'd probably just disappear.

Remember Josie, my childhood best friend? When our paths started to diverge, she hid because she didn't want me to know what she was doing, and I separated myself from her because I didn't know how to handle the tension. I spent time and energy obsessing over our differences and creating a punishing space. In the end, we built a huge gap where the winds of estrangement roared, and our gap wasn't bridged for decades. How about you? Are there friendships in your rearview mirror for which you can't quite remember how the gap began or grew?

## THE LONELINESS EPIDEMIC

As a whole, I see a cultural battle against close relationships. We're too busy. We're too far away. We're too distracted. We're too perfectionistic. And close friendships are the invariable casualty. In 2006, the American Sociological Association conducted a survey of thousands of Americans.[1] The survey re-vealed that the majority of Amer-icans say they have only two close friends. Truthfully, I didn't find that statistic sad or shocking. If there's any truth I've learned and

*One in four Americans surveyed said they don't have a single friend. Not one.*

made peace with over time, it's that we'll have only a handful of close friends with a lifelong duration. A follow-up statistic that did pierce my heart is this: one in four Americans surveyed said they don't have a single friend. Not one.

Let that sink in for a minute. If you're *not* that one in four, take a look around you. Every time you people-watch in a public place, one of the four people who pass you feels completely alone in the world. When you walk around the block in your neighborhood, behind every fourth front door there is someone living in isolation. As you stroll into church, look around you. How many people are sitting alone while you occupy your every-Sunday seat with a row of your friends or family?

One in four. I consider one in four an epidemic. As I write this, the news has been filled with the tragic Ebola epidemic in Africa. It's absolutely heart-wrenching to see video of bodies lying dead on the street unattended because of fear of the disease. It's terrible. Our hearts should be broken and moved to action.

Our American epidemic of loneliness is terrible too. Our whole country would be in an uproar with full focus on healing the sick and finding cures if our loneliness epidemic was as visible as Ebola. But it's not. Loneliness is invisible and silent, but it's still painful. You know if you're one of the one in four. You know how it feels to draw a blank if you have a bad day and try to think of someone to call. You've felt the stab in your gut of sitting at a table eating alone. Again. It's a gnawing that won't kill your body like the terrible disease of Ebola, but loneliness starves your soul.

I've felt that pain, too, so I know how you feel. I've had close friendships, but I've also experienced times of deep loneliness. I've felt the pain of feeling forgotten. I've been stung by a friend who left me feeling like I was never enough. I've been rejected by friends who didn't share my point of view. More than likely, others would say the same thing about me. I've forgotten to pay attention. I made someone feel inadequate. I rejected another because of her point of view. We've all been on both ends of the game. These experiences make us all want to run for cover—you and me both.

In my relationships, I'm sorry to say, I'm usually the one who defaults to disappearing. See, when we're clutching our lists, we know it's safer and much less messy to just withdraw behind some self-built walls and be alone. Behind those walls we can keep our personas intact and prevent anyone from getting close enough to inspect them. We can protect our battered hearts from more injury. We can lick our wounds and hide our flaws.

## COMING OUT OF HIDING

Our hearts are hungry for the intimacy of friendship. They'll starve without it. How do we reforming perfectionists replace our desire for Perfect and dive into the messiness of relationships with an open heart? Over the past decade, God has been pointing me to a woman in the Bible who reveals what's truly essential in authentic friendships. Her name is Mary Magdalene, and her beautiful friendship with Jesus teaches us what we need to develop as we strive to build our own deep, lasting friendships.

Luke 8:1–3, a short little passage, gives us a glimpse into Mary's secrets, and her secrets can help us as we get over our tendency to separate when the going gets tough. Mary didn't separate. In fact, she did the exact opposite. She sacrificed, and she stayed. Take a look. "After this, Jesus traveled about from one town and village to another, proclaiming the good news of the kingdom of God. The Twelve were with him, and also some women who had been cured of evil spirits and diseases: Mary (called Magdalene) from whom seven demons had come out; Joanna the wife of Chuza, the manager of Herod's household; Susanna; and many others. These women were helping to support them out of their own means."

Mary sacrificed to be with Jesus. First, she sacrificed her *time*. She gave up her personal agenda to hit the road with Jesus and His followers. Without a thought to what her previous life had held, her former aspirations, or the appointments written in her Day-Timer, Mary left it all to spend the rest of her days in Jesus' company. His presence was like air to her, and she was willing to sacrifice her control over her own time to be with Him. Time is a huge issue in our culture, so I'm going to come back to it and spend the whole next chapter on it. Hang tight for more on time!

But Mary didn't just sacrifice her time. She also sacrificed *social norms*. In the day in which she lived, it was highly improper for a group of women to be traveling with a tribe of men. Joanna's husband is mentioned in the passage, which may have given some respectability to her position in the group, but we aren't told Mary's marital status. It's likely that her presence was scandalous, and that leads to her third sacrifice.

She gave up her *reputation*. How can I know that for sure? Even in today's world, Mary Magdalene's name is dragged back through the mud about every decade. Remember *The Last Temptation of Christ* and *The Da Vinci Code*? It seems like Hollywood really has it out for Mary M.

## BRINGING HER LESSONS INTO OUR DAY

How can Mary's example help us as we let go of perfection and move toward better relationships? Just like her, we can sacrifice our social norms. It's normal and comfortable to be friends with women like ourselves, but some of the richest relationships grow up in the most unlikely places. Years ago when I became the women's ministry director at my church—with no experience and youth against me—my pastor liaison wisely advised me, "You need a mentor!" and he pointed me toward our church secretary. Mona was an excellent secretary, but she was so much more. She was known as our church's resident godly woman. Everyone from pastors to children sought her out for sage advice because she was known as someone who offered Scripture, which she knew inside and out, instead of her own opinion. Mona was the first contact for everyone either walking into or calling the church, and she was a consistent blessing to everyone who met her.

Feeling my own inability to fill the leadership position, I began to seek Mona out for guidance and counsel. She had a tapestried bench in front of the desk in her office, and I took my turn there as often as

I could. As I spent time with her, I learned so much more than leadership. There was a thirty-year difference in our ages, so I tried to glean as much as I could from the knowledge Mona had gained in those well-invested years. She taught me about the sufficiency of Scripture. She modeled a tamed tongue for me. She displayed grace in difficult interactions and immediate prayer when in

*An older woman who invests her life in Scripture is a treasure chest spilling gems of wisdom.*

doubt. An older woman who invests her life in Scripture is a treasure chest spilling gems of wisdom, so Mona was an ideal mentor.

## TOGETHER IS BETTER

Our friendship was rare and wonderful. Although our churches have the best of intentions, I have some serious qualms about our structure. I'm afraid we've fallen too far into the cultural pattern of dividing people into their own age groups. The children are in children's church. The youth go with the youth group. The retired folks take trips together, and the Seventy-to-Heaven class meets in a room down the hall all by themselves. Not only are we separated by age, but Sunday mornings are often described as the most segregated hour of the week. We're divided by age, race, and socioeconomics, and we are the big losers when we continually huddle in our socially normative groups.

Not only are these divisions unbiblical (take a look at Titus 2), but they also rob us of the possibility embedded in relationships with those different from ourselves. Cultivating friendships with people outside our normal circle plows our heart for growth.

In one of my all-time favorite nonfiction books, *Same Kind of Different as Me*, Ron Hall, a wealthy art dealer, and Denver Moore, a homeless man with a hidden gift for art, become fast friends. When asked about how the telling of their story has affected his everyday life, Ron answered, "I tell people all the time that I became wealthy through art but my friendship with Denver has made my life rich."[2] Jesus was the perfect example of a person who made friendships across social norms. Look at how He reached out to Mary M.—a demon-possessed woman! Ron and Denver display the beauty of living this way. We should follow.

## BE A FRIEND

As we sacrifice social norms, we'll also be called to sacrifice our self-consciousness. Although sometimes that means being looked down on by others, for perfectionists it most often means getting over ourselves, handing our personas over, and being authentic instead. I know that sounds really harsh. I promise I wouldn't say it to you if I hadn't had to say it to myself so many times.

> *I promise I wouldn't say it to you if I hadn't had to say it to myself so many times.*

During my years in women's ministry leadership, there was a woman at my church who often complained that no one wanted to be friends with her. I have to confess that although I tried to appear sympathetic, deep down I wasn't. I watched as she moved through events alone, never speaking or reaching out to anyone else. One day as she sang her same song to me again,

I had to bite back this retort: "If you *want* a friend, then *be* a friend!" Thank goodness that thought didn't make it past my lips.

Only a year later I found myself in her shoes after a move. Although I had felt known and loved in my hometown, I didn't seem to be able to connect in my new environment. I felt lonely and miserable. Going to the cross-country track meet didn't help at all. My oldest son, who was running that day, rode ahead to the meet on the bus with the team, so I showed up by myself to watch his first race. I had never attended a cross-country meet, so instantly I felt self-conscious and out of place. I didn't know where to stand. I wasn't sure how it all worked, and to make it worse, I didn't look like anybody else there either. My fluffy body, which was carefully covered in sweats from head to toe, was far different from all the lean runner bodies in cool workout clothes around me. Where did my boy get his runner gene anyway?

In desperation, I approached two moms with our high school's logo on their shirts and introduced myself. Each mom shook my hand and introduced herself in turn. "Hi, I'm Connie!" Runner Mom #1 said. "And I'm Donna," said Runner Mom #2. We chatted for a while, learning about each other's kids. Finally, I asked, "So, Donnie, how long has your son been on the team?" Both moms looked confused, then disgusted, and tried to make conversation for a few more minutes to save face before gradually moving away.

Did you get that? I did some kind of Brangelina thing with their names—morphing Connie and Donna into *Donnie*. It makes me smile now, but on that day, it further intensified my desire to dig a hole, cover myself up, and wait for the team to come thundering out of the woods and over me. I tried hard to connect. Too hard. In the trying, I became self-focused in a way that drove others away instead of drawing them in. During that awkward transition time between homes, similar uncomfortable interactions made me want to hide in my house and never come out.

Instead, I said to myself what I had wanted to say to my lonely friend: "Amy, if you want to have a friend, then *be* a friend." Then I followed that admonishment with a good talkin'-to: "Would you love a friend who took time to show that she cared by picking up the phone and asking about your day? *Then pick up the phone and ask about someone's day.* Would you love a friend who keeps confidences and is trustworthy? *Then keep a confidence, even without being asked to.* Would you love a friend who asked you to go shopping (or to the movies, or for a walk . . .) at the spur of the moment? *Then ask someone to go along when you go do those things.*"

Sometimes it's easier to stay isolated than to reach out, especially if you've been hurt or disappointed many times. I know very well. But I want to encourage you to reach out, show love, and care about others. We have to sacrifice our own self-consciousness to connect. We have to sacrifice our persona as someone who already has friends (I really think that's what most people believe about us perfectionists) and as someone who has it all together in order to be vulnerable enough to bond. Authenticity is the antidote for isolation. When we give up the social norms that keep us comfortable and the reputation that makes us feel secure, we'll find that we haven't sacrificed anything at all. It's all reward in the end.

## LEARNING TO STAY

Mary M. also teaches us how to stay. She is such a beautiful example of a constant heart. Because of her great love for Jesus, even when she might have wanted to run, she stayed. When you consider the whole of her story in Scripture, Mary M. is a picture of faithfulness:

- She stayed after He set her free.
- She stayed as He traveled.
- She stayed through His torture.
- She stayed at the cross.
- She stayed at His burial.
- She stayed to pass on the news of His resurrection.

While Mary was faithful through it all, I have trouble staying. When a church doesn't quite fit my desires, I look around for a "happier" place. When a friend is going through a bad time because of choices I can't endorse, I tend to withdraw. When God does things I can't understand, I yearn to flee to a more comfortable setting that seems easier and less painful. But I am desperate to learn to . . .

- Stay through conflict.
- Stay through struggles.
- Stay through suffering.
- Stay through discomfort.
- Stay through misunderstanding.

My perfectionistic tendencies get squeamish when things get messy, and my first reaction is to try to clean things up. In the past, I've been quick to assess situations, diagnose the problem, and tell you all about the right thing to do. Unfortunately, since I'm not actually God, people haven't typically appreciated my approach—especially since my modus operandi is to lob the "truth" and then run. (Too messy to stay for the results, see?)

## LEARNING TO ACCOMPANY

God has been teaching me a new way to live. Several years ago, I was listening to a radio show when a woman being interviewed said some-

*Since I'm not actually God, people haven't typically appreciated my approach.*

thing that echoes through me constantly. She said, "It's not my job to judge. It's my job to accompany." This truth has woven itself deeply into my heart, and it's changing me. I already know what you're thinking, because those of us who have fallen for Perfect think alike. Yes, there is a time to tell the truth. I believed that, and I still do. There are scriptural black-and-whites. God does have a standard of holiness. I value the truth-tellers in my life, and I believe I'm called to be that person for others sometimes.

Here's the problem. In those instances when I blew up friendships, I didn't generally tell the truth on God's timeline. I told it on mine. My *assessment* . . . ahem . . . maybe I should use the actual term for what I was doing . . . My *judgment* was made quickly and delivered immediately. Here's what our Righteous Judge has to say about that:

> *You, therefore, have no excuse, you who pass judgment on some-one else, for at whatever point you judge another, you are con-demning yourself, because you who pass judgment do the same things. Now we know that God's judgment against those who do such things is based on truth. So when you, a mere human being, pass judgment on them and yet do the same things, do you think you will escape God's judgment? Or do you show contempt for*

*the riches of his kindness, forbearance and patience, not realizing*
*that God's kindness is intended to lead you to repentance?*

(Romans 2:1–4)

## HOW MY JUDGMENTS FAIL

This passage points out some major problems with my assessments and judgments. My judgments are based on my limited knowledge of circumstances, while God's are based on His omniscience. My judgments are based on my biases, while God's are based on His righteousness. My judgments are based on my perceptions, while His are based on truth. My judgments are often delivered without kindness, tolerance, and patience, leading others to anger, while His kind judgments lead people to change.

## HOW HIS WAYS SUCCEED

Ouch! It hurts my heart to write such truth about the ways I've behaved in the past, but maybe you recognize yourself in those words as well. If you do, there's hope for both of us. We can change our methods and focus on accompanying instead of judging. What does that look like? For one thing, it means that no matter the circumstances, we continuously walk alongside. We live together patiently. We love constantly and lavishly. We look for our own fault in conflict. We respond humbly. And when there's sin, we patiently wait until there's nothing but love in our heart and the other heart is open. Then, without an ax to grind or our own opinion inserted, we gently discuss what Scripture has to say.

I've failed to stay so many times. I walked away from my friendship with Josie. I missed my best friend's wedding because the timing wasn't perfect for me. I've lost contact with some old friends because of hurts. In five years, four of my friends left their husbands, and though there's been some restoration since, I sank each of those friendships with quick judgments. Because of all these failures and more, I'm weary of my old ways. That weariness has stoked a passion in me for change, though, and I hope you're becoming impassioned for change as well.

Mary M. shows us that deep connections require deep commitments. I'm a woman who has shied away from those deep commitments because pain is often associated with that kind of sacrifice. But without the commitment, the level of connection my heart longs for is not possible. Think back to Luke 8:1–3. What started Mary's friendship with Jesus? He gave her everything. In a short phrase of just seven words—"from whom seven demons had come out"—we find out all we need to know about Mary's motivation for the passion of her sacrifice and the tenacity of her staying.

## FOLLOWING IN HIS STEPS

Our secular culture may not understand Mary M., but for those of us who have been set free into a loving friendship with Jesus, we get it. He's always the example, and Mary M. was just imitating what she had watched Him do. He set her free, so she lived in freedom. He connected with all He met—tax collectors, lepers, the demon-possessed, and women—so she made sure to connect deeply with Him. He sacrificed His very life to have a relationship with us, so she sacrificed her whole life to be with Him. He stayed by sending us the Holy Spirit after His death. She stayed by His side until He couldn't be found on earth any longer.

Mary M. is a woman just like us. We can only be set free to experience deep friendship to the degree that we're friends with Jesus. When we trust Him as faithful (Psalm 25:10), we won't be crushed when others inevitably fail us. In experiencing His everlasting love (Psalm 136), we are satisfied even in seasons of loneliness. As we make His name our strong tower (Proverbs 18:10), we don't need to hide behind walls to protect ourselves. Immersing ourselves in the perfecting work of His Spirit (2 Corinthians 7:1), we can break away from perfection and embrace rich, messy relationships.

"Come, Thou Fount of Every Blessing" is my favorite hymn, and I think it's because this verse resounds so loudly with me:

> O to grace how great a debtor
> daily I'm constrained to be!
> Let thy goodness, like a fetter,
> bind my wandering heart to thee.
> Prone to wander, Lord, I feel it,
> Prone to leave the God I love;
> Here's my heart, O take and seal it,
> Seal it for thy courts above.[3]

There's a part of me that has a tendency to leave or hide behind self-protective walls, but I *long* to learn to stay. My soul is created for the filling that only friendship can bring. For the sake of those friendships with God and others, I'm learning to sacrifice and develop an abiding love for God, my family, and my friends that extends a grace beyond my own strength—a strength from One who never leaves and is teaching me to stay.

## Transformation Points

1. What is your reaction when friendships get messy?

2. How has perfectionism affected your friendships with other women?

3. How would it help to learn to sacrifice and stay?

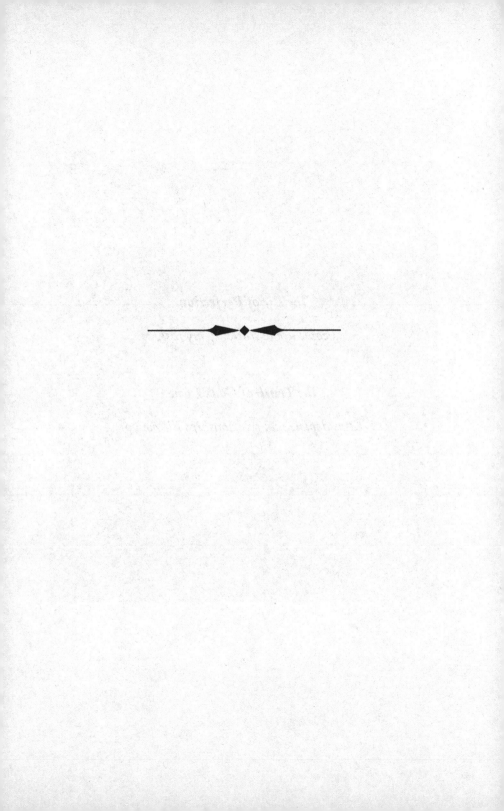

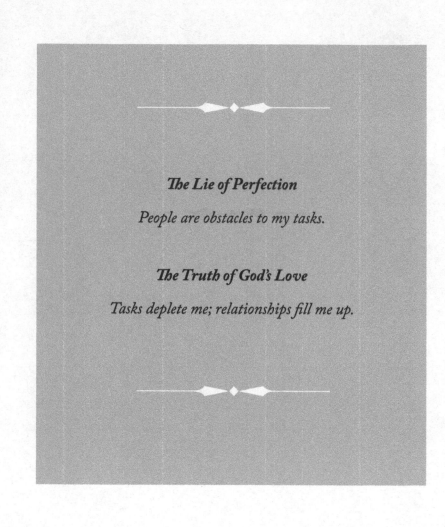

### The Lie of Perfection

*People are obstacles to my tasks.*

### The Truth of God's Love

*Tasks deplete me; relationships fill me up.*

*Chapter Eight*

# YOU WERE ALWAYS ON MY MIND

## *Replacing Tasks with People*

Hi. I'm Amy, and I'm an obsessive list-maker. Just a few months ago, I did an inventory of all the lists around my house. There was a list of people to call back on the whiteboard attached to my refrigerator. A list of movies I've missed and want to watch was lying on the kitchen counter. Still in the kitchen, I found a menu list, and I had a grocery list stuffed in my purse. Upstairs, next to my bed, was a list of books I hope to read someday. Heading up to my loft office, I found three lists on three separate legal pads of to-dos for each hat I wear in my job. When you add the inventory of my lists as a list of my lists . . . you can see the problem.

I'm such a sick list-maker that I write tasks on my lists that I've already accomplished just for the pure joy of checking them off! We perfectionists are expert list-makers, so I'm betting I'm not the only one. I'm truly a task-driven girl. Finishing a job gives me a little rush, but it's just temporary. As soon as one list of tasks is finished, another list begins.

We're busy, aren't we? Oh, so busy! Our days are filled with one activity after another. In our careers, we are driven from one project to
the next with no time for a breath be-
tween. Every season is assigned a higher
goal than the one before, without a moment to celebrate past achievements.
Almost any task you can list in our
homes—laundry, blogging, cooking,
cleaning the toilet, vacuuming the
floor—must be done and redone, espe-
cially if it's to be completed perfectly or to be used one last time to earn acceptance. If you have children, you know the pressure of having your kids involved in every activity known to man—sports practices, music lessons, children's choir, art exhibits, etc.—keeping you in a van and in the drive-through line for yet another meal in the car as you head on to the next thing.

*I write tasks on my lists that I've already accomplished just for the pure joy of checking them off!*

## THE GODS ON OUR WRISTS

Americans are infamous for our pace. We're known worldwide for our fast-food, microwave approach. Filipinos say, "Americans are people with gods on their wrists." Kenyans quip, "Africans have time but no watches. Americans have watches but no time." Hearing those quotes brings a pang to my heart that lets me know they're talking about me. Even our standard conversational responses reveal how driven we've become. Ten years ago, if you asked a friend "How are you?" the an-swer would have been "Fine." What is the response most commonly given today? "Busy!" of course.

That answer matches a competition I started engaging in years ago with a dear, godly friend. Every time we talked, no matter how the conversation began, we'd eventually begin listing the demands on our time. I'd list, and then she'd list. And then I would list more, and she would list more. On and on it went. Finally, I woke up to the disturbing trend in our friendship, and I had to ask myself some questions. What am I trying to prove? Is my busyness a sign of productivity or a symptom of perfectionism? It didn't take much introspection and insight to know the answer.

My Good Girl List had simply morphed into a to-do list. It was just another way to keep score and to measure myself against others. I began to realize I truly had a god on my wrist. My busyness had become an idol. That was the day I reconsidered busy as a virtue. With a chastened heart, I brought my apology to God, and I stopped competing with my friend. It was amazing how much our relationship improved and grew with that small choice.

That's the main problem with using busyness to fuel our idea of perfection. It damages relationships. Completed tasks hype me up, but they don't fill me up. Relationships fill me up. If I'm not very careful, I begin to believe the opposite, and people get reduced to obstacles to my tasks. I've seen a clear pattern. When busyness rises to a virtue, the fruits of the Spirit fall. Here's a little challenge for us girls with our to-do lists clenched tightly in our hands and written on our hearts. Do a measurement on a long-list day. End the day with this question. How did your love, joy, peace, patience, kindness, gentleness, and self-control (Galatians 5:22–23) hold up today? You're probably nicer than I am, but I'm telling you, those godly virtues go up in smoke on my long-list days. On those days, nothing pleasant comes out of my mouth, and this is in stark contrast to Paul's admonition to "be filled with the Spirit, speaking to one another with psalms, hymns and songs from the Spirit. Sing and make music from your heart to the Lord" (Ephesians 5:18b–19). Snapping replaces singing. Hollering usurps hymns, and screeching takes the place of psalms.

> *Godly virtues go up in smoke on my long-list days.*

When the Spirit's control begins to slip in our lives, it's usually an indicator that something besides Jesus has taken the wheel. God isn't a taskmaster. He's love (1 John 4:8). In fact, He's the loving Creator who instituted one-seventh of our lives as a mandated time of rest (Exodus 20:8–10).

First Corinthians 13 gives us a beautiful picture of the character of love, God's very essence. If we start to exhibit the opposite traits, we can know we're off track. When impatience rears its head . . . when snippiness trumps kindness . . . when we turn a nasty shade of envy green . . . when pride grips our hearts . . . when the insolent reply slips out . . . when our first thought is of our own needs . . . when rage wraps around our hearts in a flash . . . when we resurrect past mistakes . . . these are all red lights flashing to tell us that our priorities are out of whack.

## THE HEART OF THE MATTER

It happens to me most often when I have something looming that I want to be perfect—like a dinner for company or a message for a group of people I admire. I've already revealed "do-er" as part of my wiring—it may be part of your wiring too—and there's nothing inherently wrong with that trait. The world needs us do-ers to make things happen. It's not the lists or the tasks that are problematic. It's the motivation behind them. To grow in our reform, we perfectionists have to do constant, honest heart-checks about our activities. Around the time God was challenging my competition with my friend, I heard a speaker who posed a question I've been chewing on ever since. What if we could knock on the door of God's office and ask for a look at His heavenly calendar? When He opened the record of time, space, and His will, what would be written on the calendar for each of us? She then followed with an even more piercing question—what would *not* be written on it that we're currently doing anyway?

## MAYBE I NEED HEAVENLY PHONE SERVICE

I'm convinced my friend Jean has a hotline to God, because she always seems to know just what's on His calendar. She won't say yes to *anything* new on her calendar without praying about it. At first I was skeptical. I thought it was the typical "I'll pray about it" response you sometimes get when you ask someone to do something you know they don't really want to do. But after watching Jean's life for a while, I realized she really did pray about it, and she only said yes when she believed that God was saying "Yes!" Her life isn't perfection, but it's marked by those fruits of the Spirit I'm so often missing.

In reality, Jean's secret isn't a hotline to God. She uses the same resource that's available to you and me: she looks to Jesus as her example. Jesus said, "I do nothing on my own but speak just what the Father has taught me. The one who sent me is with me; he has not left me alone, for I always do what pleases him" (John 8:28b–29). Jesus is the perfect example of both productivity and peace. I've started to think of this way of living as the Principle of Intention. So often, my schedule gets out of control and my time management disappears because I live life by the seat of my pants, responding to the latest seemingly dire demand without pausing.

Just like us, when He came to Earth, Jesus submitted Himself to twenty-four-hour days in a seven-day week. Yet Jesus never lost control of His time. How did He accomplish this feat? Jesus prayed, seeking His Father's direction for His schedule. Every action and interaction. Every conversation and word spoken.

We can live the same way by implementing Jesus' Principle of Intention. As we begin our day, we too can ask the Master for a look at His calendar. God's just waiting for our request so He can grant us a peek. Can you imagine the difference that knowing His agenda will make? When my calendar is synched to God's, His provision pours into my day. But women living in the rush of perfection have difficulty setting aside time to simply listen to God. However, as we've all experienced, it's impossible to live productively and peacefully without it.

## THE ESSENTIAL PORTION

In the middle of a busy season, I woke up tired, and I knew it was going to be one of those days. I had gone to sleep with the long list of things to do rattling around in my head, slept fitfully, and awakened to the throb of anxiety. I'm sure each of you knows exactly what I'm talking about. I was facing a day with more list than time, and it seemed none of it could wait. I groaned as I dragged myself out of bed and hurried downstairs for the morning routine with my children.

Later, as I walked back into the house from the bus stop, I was tempted to skip the one thing I can't live without—time with God. "But, Lord," I argued silently, "you know that I'm dust." (Yes, that's scriptural, but also misused as one of my favorite cop-outs.) "You've given me most of the assignments on my list today, so I know you'll understand if I skip my prayer and Bible study time." Even while I rehearsed the argument in my head, I felt the draw of the One who could bring order to this chaotic day.

Scripture has a lot to say about how God feeds and strengthens His children. When Jesus was teaching His disciples, He instructed them to pray, "Give us today our daily bread" (Matthew 6:11). Notice that He didn't say weekly bread, monthly bread, or yearly bread. Just enough bread for today.

The picture I love most, though, is that of the Israelites in the desert gathering the manna God had provided as food. God's direction was to gather as much as they could eat for the day but not to try to keep it overnight. Some ignored this last part of the instruction and woke up to stinky, maggoty leftovers! (Exodus 16). God wants the same thing for us that He wanted for the Israelites. He wants us to trust Him for what we need. He wants us to be dependent on Him every morning as we face the day asking our Provider for our portion, the essential amount of strength, wisdom, and peace required. His portion is perfectly measured for our divine assignments.

In the moment of decision over how I'd start my loaded day, I remembered times I had put God off and gone straight to my to-do list. Even on those days, His grace covered my overextension, but on this particular day, I felt Him calling me to something higher. That day I made the better choice to live by the Principle of Intention. I spent some time on my knees crying out for my portion, for God's order for the day, and for a change in my own rotten attitude. Friends, I want to tell you how faithful He is! The day went smoothly, and I even had a few minutes to put my feet up, close my eyes, and thank Him before the school bus returned, bringing home my next and sweetest assignment.

## WEIGHING TIME

When we look at an overview of Jesus' life in the Gospels, the two directives of His life become clear: seek God for your portion, and prioritize people. In Jesus' economy, people always take priority over tasks. On the way to important events on His schedule, Jesus stopped to touch lepers, dine with tax collectors, and teach women. He was an extraordinary example of accomplishing His mission while still prioritizing the people He came to serve.

I have people in my life I'm called to serve while accomplishing my daily tasks. There's my husband, who needs me to close my computer and give him a true welcome when he returns home. There are my boys, who still want their mama to listen to stories of the day, though they tower over me now instead of sitting on my lap as they share. My friends deserve my time and full attention as we walk together through the days of our lives. In all my relationships, I'm learning that obedience to God's timeline is the secret to peace and even to true productivity. So I want Him to set my hours on His

*In Jesus' economy, people always take priority over tasks.*

scale of importance so they're weighted correctly. Thankfully, God has made His priorities crystal-clear in Scripture.

In John 13:34–35, Jesus says to us, "A new command I give you: Love one another. As I have loved you, so you must love one another. By this everyone will know that you are my disciples, if you love one another."

Love. One. Another. Those are three seemingly simple words with a lifetime of learning embedded in them. After all, loving others requires surrender. It requires the surrender of time and of selfish desires and motivations. During the heyday of my perfectionism, I didn't do surrender very well. I was much better at control as I managed my time, plans, and image. It may be different in your life, but motherhood was the season that broke my grip on control simply because I wasn't *able* to control any longer.

## WAVING THE WHITE FLAG

I dreamed my whole life of becoming a mom, so why was the reality so hard? As a little girl, I loved on my doll babies and swept out the play kitchen in my room. Feeding my "family" mud pies made from the sandy soil and pine needles of eastern North Carolina was my summer pastime. As I grew, helping in the church nursery was my favorite activity, and I made all my extra money with babysitting. Eventually, education became my chosen profession, and becoming an elementary school teacher just fed my love for small children.

I was filled with awe on the day I finally held my very own child. Anson Gray Carroll, my chubby infant, was born on February 20, 1994, after almost a year of trying without success to have a baby. Just as we were considering fertility treatments, a simple test confirmed the joy of conception. Anson was longed for, and he was deeply loved. I remember looking into his beautiful baby face that first day of being a mom and thinking, *Everything has changed. All my priorities have fallen into place. I'll never feel needy for anything again.*

But that wasn't true. None of the satisfying aspects of being "Mom" quenched the struggle in my soul. Despite the fact that Anson was anticipated, I had a terrible time adjusting. Suddenly, a list-making girl couldn't complete a task as simple as a shower. My schedule-loving soul resented my husband's ability to set his own work agenda while mine was set by a person who couldn't even feed himself. I was no longer called "teacher"—a job description that had defined much of my identity. What was my purpose now? I thought having a child would fulfill and perfect my life, but the world around me didn't seem to think "Mom" was a worthy title. One day I visited the school where my mother-in-law taught, with Anson in tow. When the principal saw me, he shook his head and muttered, "What a waste." He'd known me when I taught before having Anson, and he thought I'd have more value pouring my life into many children rather than just my one.

While I longed to feel the love, peace, and nurturing that seemed to come so naturally to other moms, I increasingly felt as if I were losing myself and what I perceived as my purpose. So I fought. I wrestled. I resented. I chafed at motherhood . . . until one day in the preschool pickup line when God used the title of a secular book to set me free from the struggle.

As I stood with a friend waiting for Anson (now three) and my friend's twin boys, she started telling me about a revolutionary book she had just finished. The title of the book was *Surrendering to Motherhood*. Although I've yet to read that book, I remember the conversation and the title as clearly as if it had been spoken yesterday. It was seventeen years ago, but that one phrase—*surrendering to motherhood*—changed my perspective in a moment.

## THE VIEW FROM HERE

When Anson was born, my control-freak tendencies got a chokehold grip on me. So much became beyond my power that I tilted toward anxiously grasping for control and micromanaging the joy out of life. But as I surrendered to God's timeline, I began to breathe more deeply and ease my grip. Relaxing into the crazy ride, letting the schedule flex, and intentionally enjoying the up-and-down pace of my child brought the evident benefits of surrender into view.

Before my surrender, my hands were tightly clenched as I tried desperately to hold on to control . . . and God's showered blessings fell to the ground uncaught. When I began to release my controlling ways, my hands opened wide to receive God's blessings. It was like taking a slow walk around the block, with time to admire every bug on the sidewalk along the way.

Things subtly but powerfully shifted for our whole family when God changed my mind and I surrendered to motherhood. You try it. No matter what stage of life you're in right now, you can embrace this paradigm shift. Raise the white flag. Breathe. Relax. Unclench your hands, and open them to God's blessings. Stop trying to squeeze the last drop of juice out of every minute. Surrender and enjoy. Surrender and love.

When time evaporates and eternity begins, all that will be left is relationship. There will be no more to-do lists. Only worship. There will be no more conflict about how to prioritize. We'll simply focus on the One. But we won't be alone. We'll be surrounded by all the nations, tribes, and tongues spoken of in Revelation. Included in that group will be our friends, our family, our natural children, and our spiritual children. As my husband's godly grandfather wisely said, "Relationships are the only bridge from the temporal to the eternal."

> *When time evaporates and eternity begins, all that will be left is relationship.*

## DON'T MISS THIS

Just last night as I drove through the dark alone, I flipped through the radio dial until a familiar song caught my ear. I listened to Trace Adkins sing "You're Gonna Miss This" while tears streamed down my face and dripped off my chin. The song reminisced over the phases of life, and the chorus was, "You're gonna wish these days hadn't gone by so fast."[1]

I never thought I'd miss those early days of motherhood when I was learning to surrender my time in order to love well. I do pine for them, though. The lyrics and melody of that song opened the photo album in my mind, and do you know what was there when I turned through each precious page? My mind scrolled through one face after another of the people I love. There were no pictures of a perfectly clean house. There wasn't a single one of a laundry room cleared of dirty clothes. There was no sign of gourmet dinners on perfectly laid tablescapes. Only people. Only love.

There will never be enough hours in the day to complete all our tasks, but we're all given the same 24/7. The question becomes, how will we prioritize those seconds, minutes, hours, days, and years? It's easy to throw out, "But I just don't have time to sit and listen, stop to play, pause to put on a Band-Aid, love . . ."

The truth is that the way we spend our time reveals our true priorities. Will our pursuit of perfection and our tasks rise to the top, or will we choose to surrender to love? In the end, I don't want to be known for completing my lists. I want to be known for loving God and others well. So I set time aside for needed tasks, but as I follow Jesus, I'm learning to prioritize people.

## Transformation Points

1. What is on your to-do list today?

2. Who is on your list to love today?

3. Say a prayer asking God to help you weigh the minutes and spend them correctly.

———◆◆———

### The Lie of Perfection

*Good Christian women are called to save the day.*

### The Truth of God's Love

*Only Jesus is Savior. I am called to serve by His side.*

## Chapter Nine

# YOU'RE SO VAIN

*Serving Our Savior*

There's something in me that longs to be a savior. It's the space within my heart that lights up with imagination as my TV screen shows real-life heroes who save a falling baby with a handy mattress, rescue survivors from a mudslide, or wrestle a hijacker to the floor of a plane. I aspire to be a woman with such daring. Although it's good to admire people who have acted courageously, the desire to join their ranks messes with my motives in a really negative way.

The yearning to be a hero carried me years ago on my first trip to Kolkata, India. I signed up with all the idealism and excitement of someone who had never visited a developing country. A friend who was going with me was extremely anxious, which I just didn't get. What was there to be afraid of? This was going to be an adventure! After reading books and watching videos about India, I felt completely ready. I boarded the plane bound for a whole new world and armed with assurance and bravado.

My attitude flipped, however, when I arrived in Kolkata's airport.

It was two a.m., and our exhausted team dragged our luggage through the steamy air hovering over the tarmac. My first tremor of fear started when a suspicious customs official grilled me at length, while the rest of my party waited nervously on the other side. By the time I joined the group at the doors, my confidence and courage had fled screaming.

As we walked out of the airport into the dead of night, our team was surrounded at once with emaciated, impoverished women and children who were begging when they should have been sleeping. Men, whom I later learned only wanted a tip for carrying my bag, pulled at me, invading my personal space and making me feel under attack. Decrepit buildings lined potholed streets where feral dogs, wandering cows, and rifle-armed policemen patrolled. Homeless people slept everywhere. Rancid smells and unfamiliar sights assailed our senses. Instead of feeling a sense of adventure at all the newness, I found myself shrinking into the seat of our taxi as it sped through the streets. Anxiety and homesickness consumed me.

All at once, we drove by a billboard proclaiming, "Kolkata: City of Joy." The very idea gave my brain whiplash, and my deepest motives were exposed by the first thought that popped into my head: *This is not a job for Suzy Sunshine*, I realized. *Making Kolkata the City of Joy is truly a God-sized task!*

In one brief moment, my overly idealistic notions about being a hero were exposed and crushed, and I was shoved into some realigning truth. I was not going to be able to feed the hungry, free women from oppression, or liberate captives from spiritual darkness with my bright smile and positive attitude. No, only Jesus is the Savior, and I'm simply here to experience the joy of serving Him.

*Why did I want to be a savior?* The truth was pretty ugly, although there was some good mixed in with the bad. On one hand, I desired to help people, to ease their suffering, and to introduce them to a loving God. I'm naturally wired with a compassionate heart, which Jesus has grown in me over the years. But that good was spoiled when I mixed in my desire to feel virtuous, to gain recognition from others for the "noble" thing I was doing, and to feel I had met God's requirements. Do you hear the nasty

*The works inspired by my savior complex were for my own self-gratification rather than for pleasing God.*

elements we've talked about in other chapters—the Good Girl List and a self-crafted image? What looked good on the outside was rotted with pride and vanity on the inside. The works inspired by my savior complex were for my own self-gratification rather than for pleasing God.

Some of you may wrestle different flawed motives with similar results. My friend Cheri challenged me with a contrasting perspective on a savior complex. She told me, "I have played the role of savior and rescuer in my family as far back as I can recall. I did not ask for the role. I did not choose the role. I was born into it. My brother was the rebel, my mother was chronically depressed, and my father was absent. Trying to fix everything was the *only* thing I knew how to do. It was automatic before I was ever conscious that I was doing it."

Good Girls try to be saviors because that's what they see as being good. Never Good Enough Girls try to save people because they think maybe someone will value them if they do. There's a better way for both. Jesus, our true hero and example, sets us free from the crushing weight of saving the day. He's the Savior of the highest degree. Jesus preaches good news to the poor. He binds up the brokenhearted. He proclaims freedom for the captives and releases prisoners from the darkness. Jesus brings God's favor, comforts those who mourn, and provides for those who grieve. He gives us beauty instead of ashes, gladness instead of mourning, and praise instead of despair (Isaiah 61:1–3). Jesus is beautiful and powerful and worthy of being the Savior.

In Matthew 20:25–29, Jesus reveals His Savior secret to His followers, and it's a huge surprise. It's not a good attitude, a charismatic personality, or even authority, strength, and power. The Scripture tells us,

> *Jesus called them together and said, "You know that the rulers of the Gentiles lord it over them, and their high officials exercise authority over them. Not so with you. Instead, whoever wants to become great among you must be your servant, and whoever wants to be first must be your slave—just as the Son of Man did not come to be served, but to serve, and to give his life as a ransom for many."*

The secret that leaves self-aggrandizing motives behind is *servanthood*. Through humble service to our Savior and those around us, focusing on others rather than ourselves, we can become quiet, behind-the-scenes heroes. That kind of service may not make the news, but it can definitely change the world.

## THE CHURCH THAT ALMOST HAD IT ALL

When I was growing up, a few things in our household were unacceptable. My parents were kind and loving, but some things they did not tolerate: I couldn't comment negatively about another person's physical attributes. I couldn't lay the paper napkins on the table under the forks without folding each one into a neat triangle. I couldn't use the f-word that refers to a certain bodily function most likely to happen after you eat beans. Those were the don'ts.

There were also some do's that were part of being in our family: Empty your trash can. Take your dishes to the sink after dinner. Speak kindly to your brother. (Eye roll.)

I might have given you silly examples, but rules are needed. Most of the boundaries established in my mind pertain to actions. Do this. Don't do that. And one of the things that good Christian women are supposed to *do* is serve, right? So what if our motives are slightly off, as long as we're doing good things—feeding the hungry, volunteering for our church or community, or cooking meals for new moms—right?

In Revelation, the church at Ephesus seemed to have high marks in doing all the right things and serving well. They seemed to have figured out what was acceptable to God.

*To the angel of the church in Ephesus write: These are the words of him who holds the seven stars in his right hand and walks among the seven golden lampstands: I know your deeds, your hard work and your perseverance. I know that you cannot tolerate wicked men, that you have tested those who claim to be apostles but are not, and have found them false. You have persevered and have endured hardships for my name, and have not grown weary. Yet I hold this against you: You have forsaken your first love. Remember the height from which you have fallen! Repent and do the things you did at first. If you do not repent, I will come to you and remove your lampstand from its place.*

(Revelation 2:1–5, NIV 1984)

Good deeds? Check. Hardworking? Check. Persevering? Check. Calling out wicked men and false apostles? Check. Enduring hardship in Jesus' name? Check. Not growing weary? Check. Hating bad theology? Check, check, check.

The church in Ephesus was praised by God for good works, and that's no small thing. As Jesus' followers, we're called to do good works. Ephesians 2:10 tells us, "For we are God's handiwork, created in Christ Jesus to do good works, which God prepared in advance for us to do."

But something essential was missing in that church, and the essential missing element made all the other offerings of service unacceptable. *Unacceptable* is a strong word, but God told the church at Ephesus that He'd "remove their lampstand," His blessing and Light, without it. What was this essential element? First love.

Why is love so essential to God? Without love all we've got left of our service is an external religious form. Hollow structures made only of checked-off tasks are unacceptable. What looks like service is vanity when the motive is anything other than love. The church at Ephesus almost had it all, but their works became unacceptable without the essential ingredient of love.

This scripture stabs my heart, because I've *been* the church at Ephesus so often. Those people are me. I've been the one with the checklist of rules dominating my life—including all the good things I'm accomplishing—while my heart toward God had grown cold. We girls who are lured by Perfect's web need to be on guard for certain indicators, certain flashing red lights. I know I'm in trouble when I start patting myself on the back for good results or sinking into despair for bad ones. I'm getting off track when I focus more on working perfectly than on the people with whom I'm working.

*What looks like service is vanity when the motive is anything other than love.*

Tristina, one of my blog readers, said, "I, too, struggle with this. I feel I do acts of love, but my way of showing love doesn't always translate that way to the person to whom I am trying to show love. I pray right now that God help me to show love to others the way they need to receive it."[1] Oh, Tristina, I can so relate! It's so easy to fall into service that's centered on self instead of true love.

I asked my Facebook friends how they know when their motives have gotten out of whack. Here are a few insights they shared:

- "When you start to serve with the thoughts of others having to serve you in return."
- "When you start to compare your work or load to someone else's."
- "When you start letting others know your actions."
- "When you start expecting praise or accolades for what you're doing."
- "When I expect people to notice and mention all I do."
- "When I begin to get critical of others . . . especially when things are heading in a different direction than I had planned."
- "When my feelings are hurt because someone else is asked to do something I wanted to do."
- "When it becomes duty instead of joy."

## CHECKING OUR LOVE LEVEL

Oh, ouch! Yes, indeed, those are indicators I know well. Two other sure signs we've been serving without love are exhaustion and resentment. These come after we've continued to serve with our crooked motives for some time. When we're trying to be the savior, working for perfect results in our own strength, we quickly get worn out, and weariness most often leads to resentment. Suddenly, complaining takes over. "Nobody here appreciates all I do." "I'd delegate, but no one takes the time and care over things like I do." "This _____ [fill in your act of service] sucks me dry."

Getting to this point isn't only dangerous for our own souls, but it's terrible for those we serve. In the days when I was leading my church's women's ministry, I loved the friendships I had with college girls in a nearby campus ministry. Their passion for Jesus and desire to reach out with His love to the other students on their campus was contagious. However, even evangelism and discipleship are in danger of becoming something to check off our list of Things Good Christians Do. Ailene, one of the student leaders and a precious girl, earnestly looked in my eyes one day and said, "We have to *love* people. Nobody wants to be your project." Ailene was right. Projects bring up visions of planning sessions, to-do lists, and goal assessments. Oh, how treating people as projects diminishes them to something static and sterile rather than living and vibrant. Her statement felt like

> *Treating people as projects diminishes them to something static and sterile.*

a sword jabbed into the center of me. In that moment, I got a glimpse of my messed-up motives and realized how quickly I can digress from good intentions to seeing interactions with others as an unpleasant duty. When we hear resentful comments coming out of our mouths or if people have started feeling like projects, it's time to check our love level.

We're lost without love, but God gives it lavishly. In Revelation 2:5, God gave the church explicit directions on how to have their first love restored. These three steps will help us renew our first love today, too. Let's look at the verse again: "Remember the height from which you have fallen! Repent and do the things you did at first." Remember. Repent. Return.

## REMEMBER

Step one is to remember our first love for God. To maintain the right heart, God asks us to continuously recall our first love for Him—the newness, lightness, and joy we felt when we first surrendered our lives. I think back to my ten-year-old self lying in bed, as I glowed with the newness of my first hours of salvation. Even though I had lived only a few years in sin, I felt the weight lifted, the peace of being clean, and the joy of knowing I was truly God's girl. I overflowed with a love for God and gratefulness for what He had done for me. Even now, as my mind drifts back to my first night of true Life and as I type this story for you, a fresh wave of love for God washes over me. Remembering brings a longing for that fresh first love.

## REPENT

Step two is to tell God we're sorry. It breaks my heart to think of what it means to turn away from our first love. Once we've remembered, we can see how far we've fallen. When busyness takes over, when salvation seems like "old news," when we step into the savior business, the ungratefulness and pride we feel should certainly make us weep. It's definitely something that breaks God's heart.

The only remedy is to throw ourselves at God's feet and beg for His grace. Like the tax collector in Luke 18, there are no excuses left and no words to say except, "God, have mercy on me, a sinner." Beautifully, this is right where God wants us, and it's where He can begin His transforming work. Repentance is where God takes our sorrow and makes a softened heart.

Let's *daily* and *for the rest of our lives* choose to be like the tax collector who saw himself as a broken sinner before God instead of like the Pharisee who stood in his own strength. Although one of our motives in service may be to attain a bigger, more meaningful life, working in our own strength always leads to a greatly diminished life. Luke 18 tells us it was the tax collector, not the Pharisee, who went home right with God. And when our heart is reconditioned, then we can be of use again. "For all those who exalt themselves will be humbled, and those who humble themselves will be exalted" (Luke 18:14).

> *Repentance is where God takes our sorrow and makes a softened heart.*

## RETURN

Only by turning away from sin can we return to our first love—the third step. I think back to the days when I first fell in love with my husband. I was crazy about him, and I couldn't get enough of him. I reserved every spare moment for time to be with him, and when I couldn't be in his presence, I was composing love letters or leaving voice mails. In every conversation with my friends and family, I made a way to weave in stories about Barry. I'm sure I drove them crazy! Love for him filled me with an explosive joy, bubbling over on everyone around me. Not only did I want to hug him, everybody else was in danger of being hugged, too.

If we return to our first love with God, we will embrace the things we would do at the beginning of a human love affair. We'll immerse ourselves in God's love letter to us, the Bible. We'll spend every quiet moment talking to Him and pouring out words of love, thankfulness, and praise. We'll boogie to worship music as we clean, wash the dishes, or stick in a load of laundry. Pretty soon our hearts will overflow with love for God again, and that overflow of love and joy will bubble over to those around us.

Love for God makes my heart sincere and gracious, and it keeps my motives pure. When I'm serving out of a love for God, I remember He is the Savior, and I am the servant. Beautiful results come from looking to Him alone as hero. The weight of results is on Him, while I rest in obedience. When I return to that first love, I'll want Jesus to get the accolades, and I won't watch to see who is noticing me. When my focus shifts from self, I'll be able to live out Jesus' greatest commands: "'Love the Lord your God with all your heart and with all your soul and with all your strength and with all your mind'; and, 'Love your neighbor as yourself'" (Luke 10:27).

## RESPONSIBLE FOR GIVING

Rita, a women's ministry leader, told me a powerful story years ago that still floats up into my mind when I'm grappling with a savior complex. Rita's mother, who had grown up in desperate poverty in Ukraine, was very committed to a relief project for her home country. She would collect gently used shoes from her friends, family, and community, lovingly pack them into large boxes, and ship them to an organization in Ukraine that had put out a plea for footwear. Rita's mother did this year after year as her own eight children watched and grew into adulthood.

One day, in exasperation, Rita said to her mother, "Why do you continue to work on this project? You know how corrupt the system is over there. Those shoes are probably stolen, resold, and used to line the pockets of some corrupt official. You're just wasting your time." Her mother looked at Rita with compassion and gently responded, "Rita, my responsibility is not in the receiving. My responsibility is in the giving." Ahhhh. We need a pregnant pause or a "Selah" here.

*"My responsibility is not in the receiving. My responsibility is in the giving."*

I feel a softening of the cynical places in my heart as I reflect on her mother's wisdom. There are many times when my self-centered motives cause me to hold back because I'm not sure of the return or because I'm serving only for the reward. I haven't given to poor people on the street because I didn't know how the money would be spent. I haven't freely loved some friends because I wasn't sure how they felt about me. I have withheld time from my family because I didn't think it was appreciated.

That Ebenezer Scrooge approach to life and love never serves me well. No matter what act of service we're called to, we are to be humble servants with unrestrained love. Yes, we're called to be wise stewards in how we give our time and resources, but once we've gotten our Father's affirmation, let's serve freely and with an open heart. Let's listen carefully to His voice for opportunities to give and serve because we know that He can be trusted with the results. Rita's mother exemplified our simple but not easy task to love God and love others with an open heart.

## SUZY SUNSHINE SERVES THE SAVIOR

Years after my lesson in Kolkata, I took the second trip there that I talked about earlier in the book. Remember the story of the "wedding," where Jesus split my heart open and poured His love in? Sitting on the airplane on the return flight, I reflected on all I'd learned and been given. My heart was in such a condition of overflow that I wanted to peek around to make sure none of my seatmates were getting wet from the Living Water gushing out of me. At that moment, God whispered, "It's not just women in India who are suffering, you know. Do something at home."

Once I got home, I spent months researching all the opportunities in my area. Sometimes I felt overwhelmed by the needs, but I kept asking God to show me where I could serve and learn. Finally, it became clear that God was calling me to volunteer in our county's domestic violence shelter. I signed up to begin training and attended hours of workshops until the time finally arrived for my first day "on the job."

During those days of training, Perfect tried to saunter in again with visions of broken and battered women falling to their knees in instantaneous, radical life change as I led a Bible study. I laughed at Perfect when the reality unfolded over weeks of volunteering. I may have been savior of the stockroom and hero of the heavy boxes full of donations that I sorted, but nobody fell to their knees in adoration. Before I showed up to serve, I shoved Perfect off one more time and asked God to help me show great love in small things.

That first day, I walked into my new volunteer position with my Suzy Sunshine bright smile and positive attitude. (It turns out those attributes won't save the world, but they're not bad sidekicks!) I know I'm not there to *be* a savior; instead I'm there to *serve* my Savior. Jesus is the hero; I'm just there to roll up my sleeves and stand beside Him as He serves to save the world.

## Transformation Points

1. Have you ever felt your motives souring as you served?

2. How did you respond?

3. How do you think it will change you to remember, repent, and return when you feel your love for God waning in your service?

*Part Four*

# LIVING FREELY
# AND LOVING DEEPLY

*The Lie of Perfection*

*I can't break up with Perfect; it's just who I am.*


*The Truth of God's Love*

*With God in me, I can redirect and rest in Him.*

## Chapter Ten

# RUN TO YOU

## *Choosing to Look to Him*

One of the areas of my adult life where I have definitely *never* reached Perfect is my weight. I've been Weigh Down and way back up. I've done Weight Watchers and cake watchers. I've visited the South Beach, where all the beautiful people live, and moved back inland, where the fluffy girls frolic. Most days I'm at peace with my chubbier self, but during the last year, I've been motivated to get healthier, if not thinner. In order to reach that goal, I took a foray into unknown territory.

The first time I walked into the building, I kept my head down and peered around the room from under my eyelashes. Jitters set in as I assessed my unfamiliar surroundings. The room was filled with strangers and equipment with mysterious workings, making my hands slick and my heart skip beats. I was a foreigner in a new land . . . the gym.

With a year of experience under my belt, I'm not as intimidated in my weight-lifting class as I was at the beginning, but I'm just beginning to keep up with the younger, leaner bodies. Most days. Some days I need a little push. Although my muscles were screaming for mercy in a recent class, a simple comment from my leader infused me with renewed energy. In midlift, my instructor said, "Wow, Amy. I hadn't noticed before, but your shoulders are really strong." Suddenly, my fatigue was minimized and my determination soared. Standing straighter, I completed every rep with my weights instead of skipping some like I usually do. I tried to hide the grin on my face and coolly act like my performance was no big deal, even as the satisfaction of a job well done soaked into my heart.

## GOLD-STAR GIRLS

No doubt about it. I'm a gold-star kind of girl. From elementary school days to my seasons in weight-loss programs, I'd hold my hand out with anticipation as the tiny foil stars were passed out. It seems silly for an adult to be motivated by such a trivial thing, but I've accepted it as part of my wiring. Encouragement is fuel for my tank. It makes me feel loved, stokes my fire, and energizes me for the extra mile.

Affirmation is one of the reasons we've been working so hard, isn't it? I have super-good news for you! We've been down a long, difficult road together in this book seeing the downsides of our perfectionism, but our desire to seek reward is actually a good thing. God made us this way. Others may struggle with apathy or antipathy, but not us. Our hearts are already seeking hearts. Our longing for acceptance and affirmation enables us to be extraordinarily close to God. We have a huge capacity for relationships, and that's a very good thing.

All it takes to tap into our special ability is a *subtle shift*. It's like walks on our gorgeous North Carolina beaches. You'll be charging along, watching the step ahead of you for sharp shells, and then all of a sudden, you remember to look up. You lift your chin, adjust your gaze, and the world looks instantly different. The view changes from a narrow, sandy strip to a stunning expanse of blue sky and rolling ocean. All with a subtle shift.

Most of us are in the habit of looking to other people for acceptance. We reshape our image in hopes of getting their approval. We work hard and then harder to attain their love. And all the while, God is beckoning us to lay down all our try-harder ways, lift our gaze, and look to Him.

*All it takes to tap into our special ability is a subtle shift.*

That bottomless pit in the perfectionist's heart is there for a reason. Our longing for love is a desire that God Himself wants to fill. If we'll look directly to Him for the filling, we'll never be disappointed. In fact, we'll be rewarded! Take a look at this stunning promise for those who seek Him: "And without faith it is impossible to please God, because anyone who comes to him must believe that he exists and that he rewards those who earnestly seek him" (Hebrews 11:6).

As we wholeheartedly seek God and learn to rest in His presence, we will get all the gold stars of love, acceptance, and approval that our hearts desire. And that affirmation will be from the One who is fully able to satiate our longing—our relationship-initiating God.

Our perfectionism has hindered us long enough. It's time to shift our gaze upward and embrace the deep, rich relationship our Creator offers. The wrong beliefs we've held about Him have had us cowering in fear and shame. But no more. He's already bought full acceptance for us with His Son's life, death, and resurrection. He now stands ready to bring us into a relationship with Him.

God has wired each one of us to desire the ultimate pleasure of love, and He alone is its true source. Everything else pales in comparison. Here's what Scripture tells us about God's love, a true reward and treasure:

It's unfailing (Exodus 15:13).
It's merciful (Psalm 25:6).
It's wonderful (Psalm 31:21).
It's better than life (Psalm 63:3).
It's steadfast (Psalm 86:15).
It's faithful (Psalm 89:24).
It endures forever (Psalm 118:4).
It's rich (Psalm 145:8).
It's everlasting (Jeremiah 31:3).
It's patient (1 Corinthians 13:4).
It's kind (1 Corinthians 13:4).
It's wide and long and high and deep (Ephesians 3:18).
It surpasses knowledge (Ephesians 3:19).

He beckons us to run into His open arms, where we become the comforted child, not the fix-it-all savior of our world. In His arms we are *loved*. We are *children* of God.

Those titles are sparkling stars that shine eternally. They satisfy our soul in a way human affirmation and foil-covered stars never can. God pours out His love on us for our pleasure and takes pleasure in us as we love Him. It's a beautiful cycle of lasting affirmation and the deepest pleasure for which we're all created.

## LEAVING PERFECT IN THE DUST

So let's do this thing! Let's run to God. The very nature of a race means running toward a goal and leaving the starting line behind. Although it's a process, let's make this moment the time we hear the starter's gun. I was tripped up, crippled by Perfect for way too long. Let's stop allowing Perfect to hold us back and start running toward the freedom of living in God's love right this very minute.

The year I turned forty, I wanted to do something to combat the feeling that my birthday was a marker for the downward slide. I thought and prayed about what I could do that I had never done before. Since I had never run a mile without stopping in my entire life, the goal that captured my mind, heart, and imagination was running a 5K. A marathoning friend wrote out a training plan for me, and I followed it week after week to meet my goal. The most amazing part of the process was learning spiritual truths as I ran huffing and puffing around my neighborhood. They are lessons that will help us leave Perfect far behind us forever.

## YOU CAN'T FINISH IF YOU NEVER START

When I wanted to participate in the 5K, I couldn't just Google a running plan. I couldn't simply print it, lay it on the counter, and walk by it day after day. It wasn't enough to read books about running or listen to podcasts about races. I had to run!

The place to start our race toward freedom is clear. My dear friends, true freedom begins by permanently breaking up with Perfect . . . by abandoning our quest to create the ideal life through our own strength. We might be tempted to think that Perfect is something outside ourselves, something put on us by our culture or other people. But in reality, we're our own foes.

Since we've come to understand each other so well, I'm going to say the hard thing I've been saving. It's not just an "issue" or problem to be a perfectionist. It's actually sin.

> *It's not just an "issue" or problem to be a perfectionist. It's actually sin.*

Yep. Sin. I can say that to you because I've had to face it in myself first. True perfection belongs only to God, and when we try to create it ourselves, we're pushing God out of His rightful spot. Our culture approves it and even encourages it, but we can't use "Everybody else is doing it" as an excuse anymore. We have to vanquish perfectionism, and as I've heard it said, "For this we need Jesus."

Hebrews 7 contains a challenging but amazing passage about requiring Jesus for perfection:

> *If perfection could have been attained through the Levitical priesthood—and indeed the law given to the people established that priesthood—why was there still need for another priest to come . . . ? For it is declared: "You [Jesus] are a priest forever . . ."  The former regulation is set aside because it was weak and useless (for the law made nothing perfect), and a better hope is introduced, by which we draw near to God. . . . Jesus has become the guarantor of a better covenant.*
>
> (Hebrews 7:11a, 17–19, 22b)

In the Old Testament law, the priests, or Levites, were required to work overtime to fulfill the law in order to be perfect and please God. Day after day they sacrificed animals, replaced the holy bread, and tried to honor God by following His rules. It was a repetitive and bloody business. I see myself in those priests, searching out the rules and trying to follow them with all my might in order to please God. Do you feel it too? The frustration and grief of working hard only to fall short again? The Law was given by God to reveal our need. I feel my need acutely when I'm shooting for perfection because it doesn't take long to understand the futility involved.

However, I am filled with praise when I reflect on living in a day filled with hope. In Jesus, we perfectionists can find rest and freedom from all our fruitless labor. Jesus came, sacrificed Himself, and rose again to become our forever priest. Because of Him alone, we have entered a new covenant of grace, rest, and freedom that releases us from never-ending failure. Jesus makes us fruitful as we simply follow Him. All it takes to enter the covenant with Him is a commitment to surrender. First, we make the initial surrender of our lives to Jesus—the only one who can make us perfect and restore relationship with God. Then we surrender daily and even moment by moment as we hand over our own sin of thinking we can make ourselves Good or Good Enough.

The pursuit of perfection is our particular brand of brokenness. We aren't able to break up with Perfect forever until we call our pursuit what it is. Let's do it together now. "Pursuit of perfection, you are sin!" Didn't that feel good, to tell the truth? We'll never be free until we do what the Bible tells us to do with sin. It tells us to repent. It tells us to turn away from our own efforts at fulfilling the Good Girl List or erasing the negative predictions on our Never Good Enough List. It means asking for God's forgiveness and allowing the sacrifice of Jesus to cover our sin. It is then that we receive God's grace. That's when the race toward true freedom starts.

## ONE STEP BUILDS ON ANOTHER

I wanted training for the 5K to happen quickly, but I can say it was not easy at all. To run a race, I had to spend time taking one step after another and building up my endurance. To grow as a Christian, we have to commit to spending time with the Lord and practice putting His Word into action. We don't need to be discouraged that we're not spiritual giants today, but we do need to move forward instead of being waylaid by setbacks. It doesn't matter if you're a new Christian or if you've been following Jesus for years. When we're faithful, our endurance grows.

Almost twenty years into our marriage, Barry asked an unexpected question during our family vacation that opened my eyes to some of God's difficult, progressive work in my life. Barry and I sat on a deck overlooking the ocean as we talked in low voices about the topics that concern many of us—finances, parenting, and plans for the future. Suddenly, Barry asked his startling question. "If you could change one thing about me, what would it be?"

My mind went blank except for the thought, *Whew! This is a really loaded question.* At first I didn't want to answer (why ruin a great evening?), but I finally answered, braced myself, and then re-asked the question: "What would you change about *me*?"

I had a pretty good list going in my mind of what I thought he'd say: I wish you weren't so critical. I wish you wouldn't talk so much. I wish you would cook dinner more often. What he actually said surprised me. "I want you to get your confidence back," he said. "When I married you, your favorite phrase was, 'I'll do it myself!' I've watched you lose your confidence over the years, and I want you to have it back."

He was right. Our most recent move, a few friendships with bad endings, and the struggle to find a place in my new hometown had knocked the stuffing right out of me. I had fought and lost against my tendency toward comparison, perfectionism, and an overdeveloped sense of responsibility. In the struggle to break up with Perfect, I had taken five steps forward and ten steps back. Little by little, I became convinced that I *couldn't* and that I *wasn't*. My assurance was shaken, and then it crumbled. I went from confident to crushed.

Was it God's plan that living in a new place would undo me? Did He want me to beat myself bloody after relationship disasters? No. He did, however, use this difficult place to bring me to a better place. Some

_____

*Little by little,*
*I became convinced that*
*I couldn't and that I wasn't.*

_____

things have to be torn down before they can be rebuilt. I acknowledged the past failure but used it to fuel my determination to grow. As I sought Him after Barry's eye-opening request, God began restoring me.

He spoke to me over and over again about relinquishing my picture of perfection and self-sufficiency, releasing my life to His control, and giving myself to Him for healing. He showed me what a brutal companion Perfect had been and reminded me of the promises and rewards in His Word. Promises like the one in 2 Corinthians 3:4–6 began to mend my heart:

*Such confidence we have through Christ before God. Not that we are competent in ourselves to claim anything for ourselves, but our competence comes from God. He has made us competent as ministers of a new covenant—not of the letter but of the Spirit; for the letter kills, but the Spirit gives life. (NIV)*

Like the independent do-er I tend to be, I tried attacking my feelings of insecurity in this new place with "I can do it" self-talk, but God soon brought me to the truth that "He can do it in me." He

_____

*God showed me what a brutal companion Perfect had been.*

_____

nudged me away from my own sufficiency, which is so limited and flawed, and toward dependence on His help and His Spirit's infilling power. As God did His perfecting work in me, I was folded into His love and care. Confidence in my own perfection began to fade, and confidence in His perfection opened up limitless possibilities. The hope of new possibilities helped me take one step after another back toward freedom. I'm not at the finish line yet, but I'm much closer than that day at the beach when my husband's piercing question redirected me back toward dependence on God.

## FIX YOUR EYES ON THE GOAL

One morning as I trained for the 5K, I was tempted to quit before my time was up. Weariness and discouragement weighted each step. In one last effort to endure, I focused my eyes on the trash can at the end of the track. Every step was one closer to the trash can and to the end of my run. One step. Two steps. Three steps. By staring down that trash can, I arrived triumphantly at my goal.

We have a prize to fix our eyes on that is the ultimate inspiration in life—Jesus! He is the one true and perfect man, the King of Kings, the giver of eternal life, the Beginning and the End, the Way, the Truth, and the Life. Jesus is the one who made us and knows us intimately. He created us to know Him, and He's created the way for close relationship with Him. Jesus is awesome. When my eyes are firmly fixed on Him, I find endurance and strength to run this race away from Perfect and toward His true perfection. Let's let Him set the pace and run hard after Him. Freedom is the goal. Love is the reward.

It wasn't perfect or even pretty, but I ran the whole 5K. Crossing the finish line with my face tomato red, my legs shaking uncontrollably, and my heart beating almost out of my chest, I threw my hands up in victory. Immediately, I was surrounded by my family hugging me and cheering for me. It was quite a moment. I was free of feeling feeble at forty. Even though I didn't win a medal or even get a gold star, the feeling of accomplishment was fabulous.

Nothing compares, though, to the sense of freedom and victory I feel when I run right past Perfect as it tries to shout me down. His enticements fade as I fix my eyes on Jesus and listen to His cheers. God is training my heart to trust in His provision and anticipate His prize. This is the race we were made for, and nothing else will satisfy our hearts. Breaking the bonds of perfection cracks our hearts open wide so that God can pour His love into us. Instead of failure, we experience fulfillment. Instead of exhaustion, we're filled with inexhaustible peace. Instead of hollowness, we become whole. These are the rich rewards of breaking free of Perfect and receiving God's greatest treasures.

## Transformation Points

1. Have you surrendered your life completely to Jesus?

2. If you haven't, tell Him you need Him, ask for forgiveness, commit your life to Him, and experience His love.

3. If you have surrendered your life to Him, then ask Him for forgiveness for your pursuit of perfection. Commit in prayer to run the race of freedom and ask God to give you all you need.

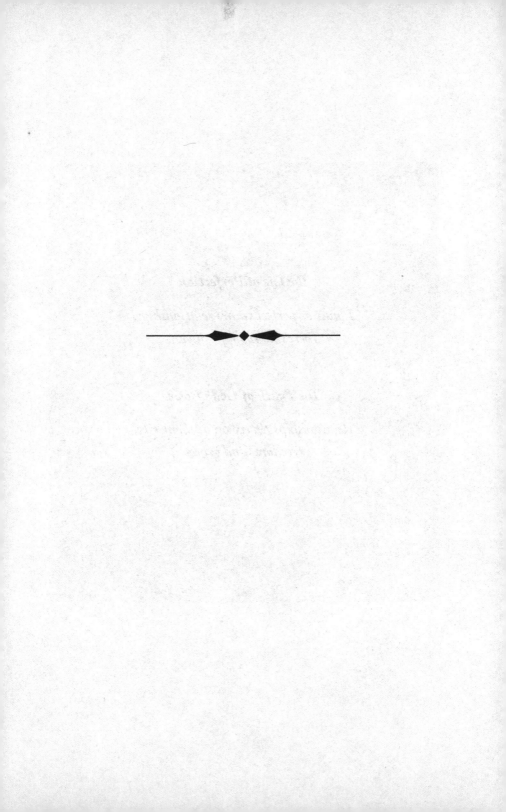

### The Lie of Perfection

*I must be perfect in my relationships.*
*There's no room for flaws.*

### The Truth of God's Love

*Relationships thrive on authenticity,*
*freedom, and grace.*

*Chapter Eleven*

# SOMEONE TO WATCH OVER ME

*Creating Relationships That Impact Eternity*

Relationship rescue. That's been my greatest need. Although it's always been true, years and years went by before my eyes were opened to the erosive nature of perfectionism on relationships. Our move eleven years ago brought it all to a head. For the first time in my life, I was lonely enough to pay attention. I was forced to slow down and look hard at my own needs. I felt the gap of not having close friends acutely; my days were no longer filled with a myriad of activities and the nearness of comfortable companionship.

God revealed my need for Him first. I look back now and see how He used it all—the move, the isolation, a trip to India, and every other moment. What was once painful is now a beautiful landscape of redemption. All of it was used. Not a bit was wasted. God was at work restoring my first love, something I sadly hadn't even known was missing. He needed me to know Him and love Him more deeply and truly before He brought me into other relationships.

During the lonely season, I may have felt alone, but I wasn't. Jesus, who has promised to be with us always, was there. My husband and children loved me with an unfailing, unconditional love. My parents and in-laws poured out love and encouragement in spite of my flaws. I've been blessed. I'm thankful that the aloneness I felt wasn't the truth. I've had people loving me and supporting me all along.

Nevertheless, I *felt* very alone, and God used that feeling redemptively. He used my flawed perceptions to create a new reality. I'm still in process—oh, I'm very much in process—but I'm not where I was. Most days, Perfect is just a memory. I've recognized the emptiness of those bad habits, and God has begun to restore my relationships. I'm grateful for my cheerleading parents (all four of them!) in a whole new way, and after years of sucking up that affirmation, I long to honor them well by being a selfless daughter. My marriage has bloomed on a whole new level since I let go of crippling expectations. Rather than micromanaging my boys, my heart's desire is to lead them to authentic experiences with God and right beliefs that will pave the way for a lifetime of growth and freedom in Him. The sunshine and rain of new friendships have fallen on my soul, and I feel as if I'm in a new place of thriving.

> *If you're not there yet, I'm simply inviting you.*

If you're not there yet, I'm simply inviting you. Don't fall into the trap of reading my words and envying the "perfection" of breaking up with Perfect. No, my life is far from perfect. And I'm okay with that . . . for the first time ever. I've come through a perspective shift rather than a circumstance shift, and it's all God's doing. He's inviting you into the same amazing life with Him.

By its very nature, perfectionism requires a lot of navel-gazing. We check and recheck our lists over and over again. We work hard to make sure every piece of our image is securely in place. We create masks and put them on in the mirror each morning to make sure nobody gets too close. We plaster our calendars with marks of activity to make sure we look good to others. We work, we perform, and we chase Perfect. Do you see how much emphasis is on the self? That's not who we are anymore! When we let go of Perfect, there's room to fold others into our arms and life.

## WORDS TO LIVE BY

Just at my breaking point, after the move when God boiled all the yuck to the top and started skimming it off, I was given an assignment to create a phrase that described my calling. Our instructor told us that our "life verse"—a Bible verse that you feel called to live by—might hold a clue. Ugh! Even though I gave my heart to Jesus when I was ten, I had never had a life verse. I'd faked one for a while here and there as I tried to fit in, but nothing ever stuck. Other Christians seemed to know exactly the verse in the Bible for them, but I didn't have any idea where to find mine.

One day as I did my morning study, a verse seemed to jump off the page at me, and then the same week it was repeated in my pastor's sermon. I'm definitely slow, but I'm not completely clueless. God made it clear that was the verse for me! I finally had my life verse. It embedded in my heart, took root, and grew. And now I present to you (drum roll, please!) Amy Carroll's life verse: "Because we loved you so much, we were delighted to share with you not only *the gospel of God but our lives as well*." (1 Thessalonians 2:8, emphasis added).

That verse has the two key components God has woven deeply into my heart: "*The gospel of God*," which is the picture of God's sacrificial love for us and the value He puts on relationships, leads the pair. "*Our lives as well*" is the part where we live out God's sacrifice, showing love to each other. It's where we live in the fullness of how we're created and in the messiness of complete authenticity. "Not only the gospel of God but our lives as well" are the keys crafted for opening our hearts wide to God and others. I hope you've heard these truths echoing all through this book. My reason for being truly lies in them.

## SHARING LIFE

A friend's compassionate call showed me how to live the gospel of God and share life in a most humbling way. "How are you doing?" she asked. "I heard about the death of your grandmother and have been thinking about you." My eyes widened in surprise and pleasure as I recognized my friend Melanie's voice on the phone. She's a friend I dearly love, but we live far from each other and don't stay in close touch.

I told her about the sadness of my loss but also of the joy over my grandmother's full life. The conversation continued as we caught up on old friends, kids, and church, but after we'd chatted for a few minutes, I started to wonder when we'd get to the real reason for her call. Finally, there was a pause, and she explained she needed to go back to her workday. I was stunned. That was it? No other agenda or hidden need was on my friend's mind. Melanie had just carved out the time in her day to call and check on me. Extraordinary.

Melanie doesn't have a lot of time to spare because she's a young widow whose precious husband died suddenly and unexpectedly. She's raising children alone, running a business they used to manage as a couple, and dealing with all the other curveballs life inevitably throws her way. Yet she made time in her day just to check in with me.

When I told her how grateful I was for her kindness, she began to explain how her husband's death had changed everything. During the week she was consumed with the business of everyday life, but worship time at church was the time when the floodgates of grief opened. She would stand and cry throughout the service, pouring out her heart to God and receiving comfort from Him. During her waves of grief, there was one woman who often sat by Melanie and silently held her hand. One woman. In silence. Offering the ministry of presence. It was a simple gesture but a profound gift. Melanie explained, "I've learned how much sharing time means. If I can only do something simple like running by and taking a cake to someone who is hurting, I do it. All of life's busyness can be overwhelming, but I make time for people now. People are the most important thing."

Do you hear it? Melanie shared Jesus' gospel with me by following His example. She gave of her time sacrificially to execute a small act of love that had big impact. She also shared her life with me. Although she is still in a period of mourning, she doesn't let the pain hold her back. She looks to the needs of others even in her grief. When she called me to join in my sadness over my grandmother, her simple act painted a picture for me of what it means to live 1 Thessalonians 2:8, while strengthening and sweetening our friendship in the process.

## MORE THAN JUST TODAY

This fresh ideal of living the gospel of God and sharing my life as well has me basking in the warmth of improved relationships, but it doesn't end there. It's not all about me or just for today. While these principles bring God's glory into our current relationships, they're in ancient Scripture to point us far into the future as well.

My friend Christie dropped a seed into my heart for growing friendships that breed spiritual multiplication. As we talked over a worn restaurant table, passion laced her voice as she leaned in to share the vision God has placed on her heart. "I want to see three spiritual generations in my lifetime," she explained. "I want to bring a woman to Jesus who learns from Him and grows in Him until she brings another woman to Jesus. When the second woman does the same, there will be three generations who love Jesus."

Fascinated, I began to scrutinize how Christie's vision shaped her life. She didn't minister to her college girls from afar. Although she was almost thirty, Christie lived in a rented house with the girls, pouring her life into them year after year. She built deep relationships and rich friendships with them to *show* how Jesus loved them rather than just *telling* them.

*Relationships are an investment into the next generation as well as a joy in our day.*

Christie stayed. Right before she turned thirty and while she was still single, God called her to an even greater sacrifice. She was called to campus ministry in Johannesburg, South Africa. I was there the day tears poured down her face as she marked "for sale" on the dishes she had been saving for married life someday. For Christie, her love for Jesus and the vision of three spiritual generations trumped any other dream. She didn't just talk about it. She lived it, and her passion was overwhelmingly contagious.

The seed Christie planted in my heart grew until her vision was mine too. Suddenly I began to view my relationships in a whole new light. They can have deeper meaning and more powerful impact when we see their value beyond just today. Our relationships are an investment into the next generation as well as a joy in our day.

## THE PICTURE MADE TRUE

I've carried the vision of three spiritual generations in my heart everywhere I go for fifteen years, so you can imagine the joy I felt when I had the opportunity to see four spiritual generations in person. I couldn't resist breaking out my camera to share the visual with you!

Let me introduce you to my precious friends. On the far left is Rita. Rita and Bobby, her husband, moved into the harsh conditions of a Hindu slum in Kolkata, India, to launch their ministry with a youth club. Week after week, Rita and Bobby showed up and set up, but nobody came. Finally, on the day they admitted defeat and stayed home, there was a knock at their door. When Rita swung open the door, there stood an angry, teenage Babita (standing beside Rita). "Where is the youth club?" she demanded. Rita explained it was canceled since no one had come, but Babita retorted, "Well, I'm here, and I've brought my brothers!" On that day, Agape Church was born, and now they have a school to reach out to the neighborhood as well. Rita is the principal, and Babita is the vice principal.

One day, a tiny girl named Merry came to school. No one in her family knew Jesus, but she craved love and learning. Babita eventually led Merry (to Babita's right) to a saving belief in Jesus, and she has grown into one of the most anointed worship leaders I've ever met. In turn, Merry has led Jaya (far right) to the Lord. In a country where being a woman is one strike against you, Jaya has three strikes: she's poor, handicapped, and a woman. But in this lineage, she's loved and accepted without reservation. This simple photograph is an extraordinary picture of grace, and I carry it in my heart as fuel for a bigger vision.

## OUR PLACE IN THE MULTITUDE

Me—one lonely woman. Melanie and her compassionate, hand-holding friend—two women joined by grief. Christie—and her vision of three women who love Jesus sacrificially. Rita, Babita, Merry, and Jaya—the picture of four spiritual generations. God constantly challenges our view. He's unfolding His bigger purpose for our relationships right before our eyes, but He doesn't limit Himself to a picture of four. He gives us an enormous, eternal view.

In Revelation 7 there's a final picture that makes my relationship-longing, nations-loving heart soar.

*After this I looked, and there before me was a great multitude that no one could count, from every nation, tribe, people and language, standing before the throne and before the Lamb. They were wearing white robes and were holding palm branches in their hands. And they cried out in a loud voice: "Salvation belongs to our God, who sits on the throne, and to the Lamb."*

(Revelation 7:9–10)

One day you and I and all our Jesus-following loved ones are going to be standing in this multitude. People of every description will be there—Dolores from Ecuador, Merry from India, and Christie from America—and we'll stand in awe to worship the One we love the most. Finally—*finally*—all relationships will be made whole without sin, flaws, or messiness. Tears rush to my eyes as I imagine the scene, and my heart beats faster contemplating the end of barriers, prejudice, misunderstanding, hurt, or any kind of false perfection in the presence of the perfect King of Kings. It will be the moment that the gospel of God and our lives are forever inextricably linked. I can't wait for that day!

God's most perfect view of relationships encompasses generation after generation of those who love Him. While our view of relationships is shrunk in the wash of our perfectionism, God wants us to have a bigger picture—an eternal perspective. Relationships matter more than anything, and since perfectionism damages all our relationships, it has to go for good.

Instead, we need to adopt a sloppy circle. It's only sloppy because it's got humans in it, but it's beautiful in Jesus' eyes. It's a circle made up of His people. He calls us to let go of anything we're holding, including our own perfection, to join hands with another. As the circle grows, we link one hand with one we love and keep the other hand free to invite those who are still coming. Our neighbor. Our coworker. Our struggling friend. Our husband. Our children. All the people around us who haven't yet followed Jesus. Our open hand is an invitation to friendship with us and a chance to know Him.

Jesus is our Someone to watch over us, but in His invitation to relationship with Him, He gives us the bonus reward of doing the messiness of this world with others. Jesus consecrates community. He blesses friendship. He lavishes love. These are the things that are perfecting our life by making us whole, mature, and complete. These are the components of the Perfect Life.

## Transformation Points

1. Who in your life has shown you how to live the gospel of God? What difference has it made?

2. Who has shared her life authentically with you? What difference has it made?

3. How would you like to build or rebuild your relationships with others based on these truths?

# FIFTY WAYS TO LEAVE
# YOUR PERFECT

Breaking up with Perfect involves both initial repentance and daily choices. To keep the process going when the book is done or to reset when you feel yourself slipping back into the Pit of Perfection, implement one or two of these a day to intentionally choose relationships over perfection. (I know. I know. It's a list. You can take the List *out of* the girl but not a list *from* the girl!) These exercises include everything from serious spiritual disciplines to the downright silly. After all, walking away from perfection needs to include lots of laughing at ourselves.

1. Go through an entire day without any form of list. Wing it and enjoy!

2. Remember that you are uniquely made and deeply loved by God. You were never meant to be a cookie-cutter woman.

3. Leave your Spanx in the drawer today and rejoice in your lumps and bumps.

4. If you don't have an answer, admit it.

5. Remind yourself . . . Your God-created personality is meant to be the beautiful centerpiece of your soul.

6. Meditate on this: "In your unfailing love you will lead the people you have redeemed. In your strength you will guide them to your holy dwelling" (Exodus 15:13).

7. Ask questions instead of pretending you know what someone is talking about.

8. Make a list of the events in your life that have shattered your picture of Perfect. Beside each, write something good that never would have happened without that event. (I know . . . I know . . . I'm asking you to do a *list!*)

9. Repeat after me: I wasn't made to pursue Perfect. I'm most amazing when I'm pursuing Jesus.

10. Pick something out of your closet you loved when you bought it, but you've never worn. (I can almost guarantee you bought it when you were feeling brave but then second-guessed whether it fit your image.) Wear it today.

11. Meditate on this: "Therefore you do not lack any spiritual gift as you eagerly wait for our Lord Jesus Christ to be revealed. He will also keep you firm to the end, so that you will be blameless on the day of our Lord Jesus Christ. God is faithful, who has called you into fellowship with his Son, Jesus Christ our Lord" (1 Corinthians 1:7–9).

12. Eat a picnic with family or friends on the floor of your most formal (translation: never used) room tonight for dinner.

13. Don't make any extra plans today and determine you'll accept whatever assignment/activity/rest God brings.

14. Remember . . . your past doesn't mean you'll never be good enough. God has determined your worth, and you are a treasure.

15. Decide today . . . I'm trading in Perfect for God's love, nurturing, forgiveness, and healing.

16. Meditate on this: "Because your love is better than life, my lips will glorify you" (Psalm 63:3).

17. Make a date with a wise, loving, truth-telling friend today. Tell her she has permission to tell you the truth about your blind spots.

18. Tell someone a story today that reveals one of your quirks and laugh about it.

19. Intentionally plan a time of rest.

20. Start a journal where you record truths about God's character as you read the Bible.

21. Meditate on this: "Teach us to number our days, that we may gain a heart of wisdom" (Psalm 90:12).

22. Say this out loud: "I will stop my pursuit of perfection so God can begin perfecting me."

23. Wear mismatched socks on purpose. Don't tell anybody, but giggle every time you think about it during the day.

24. Remind yourself: your identity is in Christ, not the roles you fill.

25. If you have kids, let them wear whatever they want to school today. Or paint your fingernails a wild color just for fun.

26. Meditate on this: "But he said to me, 'My grace is sufficient for you, for my power is made perfect in weakness.' Therefore I will boast all the more gladly about my weaknesses, so that Christ's power may rest on me" (2 Corinthians 12:9).

27. Rejoice in God's greatness and your smallness.

28. Invite friends over on the spur of the moment. You're allowed to wipe down the downstairs bathroom but not to clean the whole house!

29. Examine a conflict you've been part of recently. How did it start? Was it because your expectations weren't met? Take a step to restore that relationship.

30. Identify one unrealistic expectation you have of someone you love. Let it go.

31. Meditate on this: "And I pray that you, being rooted and established in love, may have power, together with all the Lord's holy people, to grasp how wide and long and high and deep is the love of Christ, and to know this love that surpasses knowledge—that you may be filled to the measure of all the fullness of God" (Ephesians 3:17b–19).

32. Let your kids pack their own lunch today or pack a Twinkie for your snack break at work. (One day won't hurt, and we all deserve to act like kids sometimes!)

33. Assign someone in your group to make all the decisions for the night out. Go along for the ride.

34. Be honest with yourself about someone of whom you've been jealous. Pray blessings over his or her gifts.

35. Choose to put someone else first as you go through your day today.

36. Meditate on this: "For by one sacrifice he [Jesus] has made perfect forever those who are being made holy" (Hebrews 10:14).

37. Look for an opportunity to let someone else have their way even when you're convinced your way is best.

38. Identify something you've used to create an image—a piece of clothing, an accessory, an activity, etc.—that doesn't match who you really are. Get rid of it, and replace it with something that's true to you.

39. Be aware of when you start striving for perfection today. Remind yourself to turn to God, pray, and rest in His perfecting work.

40. Don't make your bed today. Jump on it if you dare!

41. Meditate on this: "There is no fear in love. But perfect love drives out fear, because fear has to do with punishment. The one who fears is not made perfect in love" (1 John 4:18).

42. Choose a spiritual activity today that will increase your internal being—prayer, Bible study, scripture memorization, silence/listening to God—instead of worrying about the externals.

43. Sign up to volunteer serving a group of people very different from you.

44. Instead of going shopping with a friend today, plan a fun activity that focuses on relationships. (E.g., I'm celebrating with friends soon by buying some Depends and heading to a trampoline park!)

45. Clean out your closet with an eye for excess. Give the items away to your favorite charity with a thrift store or leave them anonymously on the porch of a friend who you know would be blessed and delighted.

46. Meditate on this: "Now to him who is able to do immeasurably more than all we ask or imagine, according to his power that is at work within us, to him be glory in the church and in Christ Jesus throughout all generations, for ever and ever! Amen" (Ephesians 3:20–21).

47. Think through relationships you've ended over the years. Do you have regrets because you severed them when things just got too uncomfortable for you? Reach out to those friends with a card or e-mail.

48. Take your calendar into your time with God. Ask Him to verify or correct your schedule.

49. Assess your service. Is your love tank overflowing into your tasks?

50. Meditate on this: "Not that I have already obtained all this, or have already been made perfect, but I press on to take hold of that for which Christ Jesus took hold of me.... But one thing I do: Forgetting what is behind and straining toward what is ahead, I press on toward the goal to win the prize for which God has called me heavenward in Christ Jesus" (Philippians 3:12, 13b–14, NIV 1984).

# GOING DEEPER

This section of the book is for those who want to go a bit deeper into the concepts presented in the preceding pages. It's something that will work for individual reflection as well as for group study. I love writing in a pretty journal as I'm processing new concepts. The "pretty" is optional, but do have a specific notebook or journal where you can write your thoughts about your breakup with perfection. Where I ask you to mark up specific scriptures, I've printed those scriptures in this section; all other scriptures are referred to by their references, and you can look them up in your Bible.

## INTRODUCTION: BREAKING UP IS HARD TO DO

1. Read these stories of Jesus' interactions with others, and answer the questions for each.

- Mark 5:25–34 (Woman with the issue of blood)
  - What personality trait(s) can you see in the person interacting with Jesus?
  - What personality trait(s) does Jesus display?
  - How is this person changed by their encounter with Jesus? Were they freed? Why or why not?

- Luke 19:1–10 (Zacchaeus)
  - What personality trait(s) can you see in the person interacting with Jesus?
  - What personality trait(s) does Jesus display?
  - How is this person changed by their encounter with Jesus? Were they freed? Why or why not?

- Mark 10:17–22 (Rich young man)
  - What personality trait(s) can you see in the person interacting with Jesus?
  - What personality trait(s) does Jesus display?
  - How is this person changed by their encounter with Jesus? Were they freed? Why or why not?

2. Make a list of any personality traits that keep you from living freely.

3. Write a prayer to Jesus asking Him to straighten any warps in your personality and asking Him to use them for His glory.

4. Read these stories of Jesus' encounters with others, and answer the questions for each.

- John 4:3–29 (woman at the well)
  - What event in this person's past kept them from a joyful life?
  - What words did Jesus speak about his/her past?
  - How did Jesus' words change his/her future?

- John 8:3–11 (adulterous woman)
  - What event in this person's past kept them from a joyful life?

- What words did Jesus speak about his/her past?
- How did Jesus' words change his/her future?


- Luke 22:54–62, John 21:4–19 (Peter after denying Jesus)
  - What event in this person's past kept them from a joyful life?
  - What words did Jesus speak about his/her past?
  - How did Jesus' words change his/her future?

5. Make a list of any things in your past that make you doubt God could love you completely.

6. Write a prayer asking Jesus to forgive you fully and to help you walk in complete freedom.

## CHAPTER 1: WHAT A FOOL BELIEVES

**Note: This is intended to be a gut-wrenchingly honest exercise. No holding back or Sunday school answers allowed.

1. If you hold the Good Girl List, write down all the things you believe you need to do to earn God's love.

2. If you hold the Never Good Enough List, write down all the things you've done that you believe keep God from loving you.

3. Read these truths from the scriptures below. Circle two that most resonate with you. When you're ready, pray and tell God you're ready to give up your list. Get a colored pen or marker and write the truths you've circled over the list you wrote out

in questions 1 and 2. (Warning: The following truths could change your life if you believe them.)

**Romans 8:38–39, NIV:** *For I am convinced that neither death nor life, neither angels nor demons, neither the present nor the future, nor any powers, neither height nor depth, nor anything else in all creation, will be able to separate us from the love of God that is in Christ Jesus our Lord.*

**John 15:9, NIV:** *As the Father has loved me, so have I loved you. Now remain in my love.*

**Exodus 34:6b–7a:** *The LORD, the LORD, the compassionate and gracious God, slow to anger, abounding in love and faithfulness, maintaining love to thousands, and forgiving wickedness, rebellion and sin.*

**Psalm 13:5–6:** *But I trust in your unfailing love; my heart rejoices in your salvation. I will sing the LORD's praise, for he has been good to me.*

**Titus 3:4–5:** *But when the kindness and love of God our Savior appeared, he saved us, not because of righteous things we had done, but because of his mercy. He saved us through the washing of rebirth and renewal by the Holy Spirit.*

**Matthew 9:13:** *But go and learn what this means: "I desire mercy, not sacrifice." For I have not come to call the righteous, but sinners.*

**Psalm 103:2–5:** *Praise the* LORD, *O my soul, and forget not all his benefits—who forgives all your sins and heals all your diseases, who redeems your life from the pit and crowns you with love and compassion, who satisfies your desires with good things so that your youth is renewed like the eagle's.*

**2 Peter 1:3:** *His divine power has given us everything we need for a godly life through our knowledge of him who called us by his own glory and goodness.*

4. Set aside a few pages in your journal, titled "Who God Says He Is." As you read your Bible, list truths about God that you discover, along with the scripture reference. For example . . .

**Exodus 34:6:**
- God is the Lord.
- He is compassionate and gracious.
- God is slow to anger.
- He is abounding in love and faithfulness.
- (Don't you just love this passage? It's God's ultimate definition of Himself!)

## CHAPTER 2: DUST IN THE WIND

Messages about Martha usually stop with the first scene of her story, the famous scene where her sister Mary makes the right choice and Martha bombs.

*But* . . . the story doesn't end there. In Jesus' response to Martha, I hear kindness and a winsome invitation. I strongly believe that Martha accepted Jesus' invitation to sit at His feet to learn, because in the next scene, we get to see Martha's personality redeemed. If there's a place for Marys at Jesus' feet, He'll make a place for Marthas too.

1. Reread the story told in this chapter from Luke 10:38–42. Write down any additional observations you have from this story.

2. Now read John 11:1–44, then answer the questions below:
   • What did Martha do when she heard Jesus was coming?
   • How is this response different than in the scene where we first met Martha?
   • What truths about Jesus does she speak?
   • Where do you think she learned such profound truth?
   • How would you describe the change in Martha from the Luke passage to the one described in John?
   • How do these stories make you feel as a woman who struggles with perfection? Do you have greater hope for personal change?

## CHAPTER 3: IT'S NOT YOU, IT'S ME

1. Hannah's is a beautiful story about a woman who expectantly sought God. Read her story in 1 Samuel 1:1–2:11.

2. From verses 1:1–1:8, make a list of things you learn about the circumstances of Hannah's life.

3. During this time period, women were expected to bear children. A man, a woman, and a passel of children were thought to be the perfect family. More than that, children were thought to be a sign of God's blessing. What clues do we see about how Hannah may have felt under the weight of expectation?

4. What expectations weigh you down?

5. Who might Hannah have blamed for her lack of children and her feelings about her barrenness? What other internal ugliness might have risen up in Hannah? Comparison? Covetousness?

6. Is there anyone you blame for your unmet or unrealistic expectations?

7. In a nutshell, describe Hannah's response to her unmet expectations.

8. How did God meet Hannah in her disappointment?

9. Do you see the solution as perfect or flawed?

10. How do you sense God meeting you in your disappointment, blame, covetousness, or comparison?

## CHAPTER 4: PAPER DOLL

1. Read 1 Corinthians 1:26–31.

2. In verse 26, what traits are listed that humans value?

3. Do you see yourself using any of these to shape your image?

What are some of the roles you've used or things you've done to shape your image?

4. In verses 27–28, God reveals the kind of traits He chooses. Make a list of them.

5. What does verse 29 tell us about why He chooses those things?

6. Verse 30 tells us that we can be "in Christ." Amazing, right? How might being in Christ and bearing God's image be the same? Different?

7. What gifts do we receive when we're in Christ? How would those gifts change your image and identity?

## CHAPTER 5: HEARTBREAK HOTEL

1. Read 1 Kings 3:1–14.

2. Why did God appear to Solomon in a dream and offer whatever he asked?

3. Alongside your translation, read verse 9 from The Message: "Here's what I want: Give me a God-listening heart so I can lead your people well, discerning the difference between good and evil. For who on their own is capable of leading your glorious people?" (1 Kings 3:9, The Message)

4. What did Solomon request of God? What reason did he give?

5. What could Solomon have requested?

6. What do you think Solomon's choice reveals about his heart? How did his "wanter" reveal what he loved?

7. If you were given a choice from God as amazing as Solomon's, what would you ask for? (Be honest!) What does that choice reveal about your heart and what you love?

8. Write a prayer asking God to adjust your wanter if it needs adjustment. Ask Him to show you practical steps to cut off anything you love more than Him.

## CHAPTER 6: WE ARE NEVER GETTING BACK TOGETHER

The book of Psalms is amazing in that it unapologetically reflects the entire range of human emotion. We perfectionists tend to shut down our emotions so we can plow through our circumstances, never allowing ourselves to feel our needs. But Psalms 4 can help us reverse this trend. In this psalm, David expresses the three steps of building relationship through *feeling need*, *acknowledging need*, and *receiving*. Read the passage below and then work through the questions that follow.

### Psalm 4

*Answer me when I call to you,*
    *my righteous God.*
    *Give me relief from my distress;*
    *have mercy on me and hear my prayer.*
    *How long will you people turn my glory into shame?*
    *How long will you love delusions and seek false gods?*

*Know that the Lord has set apart his faithful servant for himself;*
    *the Lord hears when I call to him.*
*Tremble and do not sin;*
        *when you are on your beds,*
        *search your hearts and be silent.*
*Offer the sacrifices of the righteous*
        *and trust in the Lord.*
*Many, Lord, are asking, "Who will bring us prosperity?"*
        *Let the light of your face shine on us.*
*Fill my heart with joy*
        *when their grain and new wine abound.*
*In peace I will lie down and sleep,*
        *for you alone, Lord,*
        *make me dwell in safety.*

1. With a straight line, underline the places where David expresses his emotions.

2. With a wavy line, underline the places where David expresses his needs and makes requests.

3. Circle what David receives from the Lord. (There is some overlap between the three steps, so don't worry about doing it perfectly!)

4. What are some of the emotions you feel when you put perfection aside?

5. Make a list of the needs you have that you can't or shouldn't fill yourself.

6. Is there someone in your life who would be willing to help you?

7. What might change in your relationship with that person and others, if you received help?

8. Write a prayer crying out to God for the things only He can give. Ask Him to help you reach out for help from your friends and family when you need it.

## CHAPTER 7: ALL BY MYSELF

Let's take a look at a familiar story with fresh eyes—eyes that are looking at the idea of sacrifice and staying in a friendship.

1. Read Luke 1:5–25.

   • Who was Zechariah? How did his standing affect Elizabeth?
   • What was the dilemma this couple faced?
   • What did the angel tell Zechariah? What was Zechariah's reaction to the news?
   • What was Elizabeth's reaction to her pregnancy? What does her reaction tell you about her character?

2. Read Luke 1:26–38.

   • What did Mary's reaction to the news of her pregnancy tell you about her?

3. Read Luke 1:39–56.

- What does Elizabeth's reaction to Mary's news tell us about why Mary may have wanted to be with her?
- Most theologians believe Mary was a teenager. What does her status versus Elizabeth's status tell you about Elizabeth's reaction? What did Elizabeth sacrifice in that reaction?
- How long did Mary stay with Elizabeth? What are some of the possible challenges of two pregnant women living together for that length of time? What are some of the possible blessings?

## CHAPTER 8: YOU WERE ALWAYS ON MY MIND

One of the beautiful benefits of surrender is rest—both internal and physical peace. As you read through these scriptures about rest, consider the following:

1. Circle the three verses that speak to you personally.

2. List in your journal the new things you learn about rest.

3. Ask yourself what you need to change about the way you spend your time to prioritize the gift of rest.

**Exodus 20: 8–11:** *Remember the Sabbath day by keeping it holy. Six days you shall labor and do all your work, but the seventh day is a Sabbath to the LORD your God. On it you shall not do any work, neither you, nor your son or daughter, nor your male or female servant, nor your animals, nor any foreigner residing in your* *towns. For in six days the LORD made the heavens and the earth, the sea, and all that is in them, but He rested on the seventh day. Therefore the LORD blessed the Sabbath day and made it holy.*

**Exodus 33:14:** *The LORD replied, "My Presence will go with you, and I will give you rest."*

**Joshua 21:44:** *The LORD gave them rest on every side, just as he had sworn to their ancestors. Not one of their enemies withstood them; the LORD gave all their enemies into their hands.*

**1 Kings 8:56:** *Praise be to the LORD, who has given rest to his people Israel just as he promised. Not one word has failed of all the good promises he gave through his servant Moses.*

**Psalm 62:1:** *Truly my soul finds rest in God; my salvation comes from him.*

**Psalm 91:1:** *Whoever dwells in the shelter of the Most High will rest in the shadow of the Almighty.*

**Psalm 116:7:** *Return to your rest, my soul, for the LORD has been good to you.*

**Isaiah 30:15:** *This is what the Sovereign LORD, the Holy One of Israel, says: "In repentance and rest is your salvation, in quietness and trust is your strength, but you would have none of it."*

**Matthew 11:28–29:** *Come to me, all you who are weary and burdened, and I will give you rest. Take my yoke upon you and learn from me, for I am gentle and humble in heart, and you will find rest for your souls.*

**Hebrews 4:3:** *Now we who have believed enter that rest, just as God has said, "So I declared on oath in my anger, They shall never enter my rest." And yet his works have been finished since the creation of the world.*

**Hebrews 4:9–10:** *There remains, then, a Sabbath-rest for the people of God; for anyone who enters God's rest also rests from his own works, just as God did from his.*

## CHAPTER 9: YOU'RE SO VAIN

1. Read John 13:3–9.

2. What does verse 3 tell us about why Jesus washed His disciples' feet?

3. What further explanation does verse 8 give?

4. What are some of the words you'd use to describe Jesus as He washed His friends' feet?

5. What are some of the motives that trip you up as you serve?

6. How could you increase your love for God as you serve?

7. How should we follow Jesus' example of service?

## CHAPTER 10: RUN TO YOU

Read Luke 15:11–32, then answer the following questions:

1. What did the youngest son see as the perfect plan for his life at the beginning of the story?

2. When did he change his mind?

3. What did he do?

4. How did his father respond?

5. Since this is a picture of how our heavenly Father responds to us, what is happening when we turn around from our pursuit of perfection and come home to our Father?

6. How does this knowledge that God is running toward you while you are running toward Him change your attitude about repentance?

## CHAPTER 11: SOMEONE TO WATCH OVER ME

1. Read Titus 2.

   • What relationships do you see listed?

2. Reread verses 5, 8, 10, and 12.

   • What are the purposes given for the relationships in this chapter?
   • How do these purposes give you new direction for your existing relationships?
   • For new ones you form in the future?

# ACKNOWLEDGMENTS

Writing is an isolating task by nature. After sequestering myself to write this book, my extroverted soul craved community, so I'm more thankful than ever for my family and friends. I love you. I need you. I'm sorry if I sucked you dry when I finally descended from my office to grab some face time.

Barry, Anson, and Nolan—I am the luckiest woman alive to be the lone girl hangin' with the boys. I love our life together and the way you fill our home with music and laughter.

Mom, Dad, Barbara, and Barry—we don't get to control who our parents are, but if I got to pick, I'd pick you. Your constant love and encouragement fuel my fire.

Holly Ladner, Brigitte Harrison, Tara Furman, and all my precious girlfriends old and new—after a stretch of loneliness, I know for sure I don't ever want to do life without you. It's just not as fun! Let's do coffee next week.

The Proverbs 31 team—I know I'm in the right place because of your passionate commitment to grow in God while transparently sharing our journeys' fumbles. Thank you for the shared wisdom, the bottomless well of encouragement, and the determination to show the world that a group of women really can get along and get things done! Lysa, I love following your God-focused leadership.

My Connections Class sisters—I'm so grateful for our eclectic group that loves exceedingly well. You prayed for this book before it was even born. You buoyed me when I was sinking. You believed in me more than I believed in myself. Thank you. Carol Byrd, I love partnering with you and sitting under your teaching, friend.

Pastor John Mark Harrison and Apex Baptist Church—oh, how I love the family we've formed. I'm yours, and I'm so glad you're mine. It's an honor to walk through the messiness of everyday life with you, and I'm simply amazed as Jesus shows off in our midst.

Amy's Go-To Girls—just when I was sinking into despair, you joined me in the writing process and gave me hope and help. Special thanks to Megan Dohm, my dear niece; Janet Dohm, my sis-in-law; Wendy Schultz; Sheila Mangum; and Cheri Gregory, who invested countless hours and brain cells to help shape the book we hold in our hands.

Cara's Writer Group—y'all nurtured the dream and kept it alive. I can't wait to hold your books in my hands.

Blythe Daniel—you're the best agent a girl could have. You went above and beyond in helping to shape the proposal that launched this book process. You pushed me beyond what I thought I could do with all the love and gentleness of your nature. Thank you. (Even though I was a mess at the time. Pushing a perfectionist is a harrowing process!)

Philis Boultinghouse and Howard Books—I was a reluctant writer because of fear. I knew this first-time author wouldn't do it perfectly, but your belief in me and this book is a precious treasure I hold in my heart.

Jesus—without You, I'd be a lost and lonely mess. Thank You for extravagantly loving this imperfect girl, lavishly pouring out Your grace, and gently moving me closer to You every day. I'm still watching what You do with wide-eyed wonder.

# NOTES

## Chapter 2: Dust in the Wind

1. Barna Group, "Christian Women Today, Part 3 of 4: A Well-Being Check-Up," August 21, 2012, https://www.barna.org/culture-articles/587-christian-women-today-part-3-of-4-women-give-themselves-an-emotional-and-spiritual-check-up.

2. Louie Giglio, *I Am Not but I Know I AM* (Colorado Springs, CO: Multnomah Books, 2005), 20.

## Chapter 3: It's Not You, It's Me

1. Lysa TerKeurst, *The Best Yes: Making Wise Decisions in the Midst of Endless Demands* (Nashville, TN: Nelson Books, 2014), 120.

2. J. P. Louw and E. A. Nida, *Greek-English Lexicon of the New Testament: Based on Semantic Domains* (New York: United Bible Societies, 1996).

## Chapter 4: Paper Doll

1. Statista, "Number of monthly active Facebook users worldwide," accessed February 2015, http://www.statista.com/statistics/264810/number-of-monthly-active-facebook-users-worldwide/.

2. Statistic Brain, "Facebook Statistics," July 1, 2014, http://www.statisticbrain.com/facebook-statistics/.

3. Ben Parr, "The First Thing Young Women Do in the Morning: Check Facebook," *Mashable*, July 6, 2010, http://mashable.com /2010/07/07/oxygen-facebook-study/.

## Chapter 5: Heartbreak Hotel

1. Tori DeAngelis, "Consumerism and Its Discontents," *American Psychological Association Monitor on Psychology* 35, no. 6 (June 2004), http://www.apa.org/monitor/jun04/discontents.aspx.

2. Jen Hatmaker, *7* (Nashville, TN: B & H Publishing Group, 2012), 91.

3. My Budget 360, http://www.mybudget360.com/how-much-do -americans-earn-what-is-the-average-us-income/.

4. Anup Shah, "Poverty and Statistics," *Global Issues*, January 7, 2013, http://www.globalissues.org/article/26/poverty-facts-and-stats.

5. Richard Stearns, *The Hole in Our Gospel* (Nashville, TN: Thomas Nelson, 2010), 122.

## Chapter 7: All by Myself

1. American Sociological Association, "Americans' Circle of Friends Is Shrinking," press release, June 16, 2006, http://www.asanet.org/ press/20060616.cfm.

2. Ron Hall and Denver Moore with Lynn Vincent, *Same Kind of Different as Me* (Nashville, TN: Thomas Nelson, 2006), 241.

3. Robert Robinson, "Come, Thou Fount of Every Blessing," *A Collection of Hymns Used by the Church of Christ in Angel Alley, Bishopsgate*, 1759.

## Chapter 8: You Were Always on My Mind

1. Trace Adkins, "You're Gonna Miss This," by Ashley Glenn Gorley and Lee Thomas Miller, on *American Man: Greatest Hits 2*, Warner /Chappell Music Inc. and EMI Music Publishing, 2007.

## Chapter 9: You're So Vain

1. Tristina Senter, February 7, 2014, 11:14 a.m., comment on Amy Carroll, "Unacceptable," *Amy Carroll* (blog), February 6, 2014, http://amycarroll.org/unacceptable/. Used by permission.

# ABOUT THE AUTHOR

Amy Carroll's most cherished titles are wife, mom, daughter, and friend. Her position on the Proverbs 31 Ministries Speaker Team allows her to tell about her closest friend, Jesus, to new pals all across the nation. Needless to say, it's a job, even after close to a decade, that continues to thrill her soul.

Amy's passion is living the untied life. She loves to see women freed into the matchless pleasure of deep relationship with God and others.

Committing to open up her whole life (the good, the bad, *and* the ugly) allows her to teach the lessons she's learned in her pursuit of applying God's truth. Her background as an educator has enhanced her God-given ability to share His big truths in small, understandable bites.

Amy writes devotions for Proverbs 31 Ministries' Encouragement for Today e-mails, which are sent out daily to over 750,000 people worldwide. She is a contributing author for the *NIV Real-Life Devotional Bible for Women* and *Encouragement for Today.* Amy also is the director and coach of Next Step Speaker Services, a coaching service for Christian speakers.

She lives in North Carolina with her three favorite guys and a little red dachshund. You can find her on any given day typing at her computer, reading a book, or trying to figure out one more alternative to cooking dinner.

To connect with Amy, visit her at . . .

Her website and blog: www.amycarroll.org
Facebook: Amy Dohm Carroll
Twitter: @amycarrollp31
Proverbs 31 Ministries: www.proverbs31.org

To inquire about having Amy speak for your next event, visit http://proverbs31.org/speakers/inquire-about-our-speakers/ or call the Proverbs 31 Ministries office at 1-877-731-4663.

**Proverbs 31**
MINISTRIES

# ABOUT PROVERBS 31 MINISTRIES

Amy Carroll is an author, speaker, and online devotion writer for Proverbs 31 Ministries, located in Charlotte, North Carolina.

If you were inspired by *Breaking Up with Perfect* and desire to deepen your own personal relationship with Jesus Christ, I encourage you to connect with Proverbs 31 Ministries.

We exist to be a trusted friend who will take you by the hand and walk by your side, leading you one step closer to the heart of God through:

- Free online daily devotions
- Online Bible studies
- Daily radio programs
- Books and resources

For more information about Proverbs 31 Ministries, visit:
www.Proverbs31.org.